Roots, Renewal and the Brethren

nathan delynn smith

foreword by

c. donald cole

HOPE
Publishing House
P.O. Box 60008
Pasadena, CA 91106

Copyright © 1986 by
Hope Publishing House
P.O. Box 60008
Pasadena CA 91106

Printed in the U.S.A.

Manuscript editor: Faith Annette Sand

Illustrator: Erika Oller

Library of Congress Cataloging in Publication Data

Smith, Nathan DeLynn, 1937-
  Roots, Renewal and the Brethren.

Originally presented as the author's thesis (Doctor of Ministry—
Fuller Theological Seminary)
  Bibliography: p.
  1. Plymouth Brethren. 2. Church renewal—Plymouth Brethren.
I. Title.

BX8800.S56 1986 289.9 86-7136
ISBN 0-932727-09-3
ISBN 0-932727-08-5 (paperback)

CONTENTS

Foreword

This is a brave book. It is also a wounding book, because it lists the failings of a fine group of people. They want to please God, and to hear that their church practices are inadequate will surely cause them pain. But the author loves the people whose practices he criticizes. Therefore, the wounds he gives are the wounds of a friend. The wounds of a friend, Solomon says, "can be trusted" (Proverbs 27:6, NIV). Solomon may have learned that from his father David. "Let a righteous man strike me—it is a kindness," David said. "Let him rebuke me—it is oil on my head" (Psalm 141:5). David ends that prayer with a promise: "My head will not refuse it."

Some of Nate Smith's readers may refuse whatever rebuke may be implicit in the book. That would be a pity! What the author says is worth hearing. Nate's love for the Brethren and his vast experience among them give him the moral qualifications needed for the task to which he set himself. His training as a scholar and years of classroom teaching give him the necessary academic credentials. His book can be read with confidence; it isn't a sleazy expose of insincere people. It's a thoughtful book, written by a competent scholar whose love and respect for the people concerned is never in doubt.

If the book were just a list of the sins of the Brethren, real or imagined, it wouldn't be worth much. It takes neither talent nor effort to criticize, and no denomination is without fault. If Nate Smith had wanted to write—one of those books that lays bare everything that is bad in a church—he'd have taken on bigger game than the Brethren. But mere criticism is not his objective, except for the reason that Paul dealt sharply with his friends in Corinth: "In the following directives I have no praise for you, for your meetings do more harm than good" (1 Corinthians 11:17). How thankful we are for what follows that stinging rebuke—rich insights into the meaning of the Lord's Supper.

This is not only a brave book, it is also a helpful book—for those who are willing to be helped and have the courage to make whatever changes may be needed. Courage will be required. Make no mistake about that. But the results will make it worthwhile—to the glory of God in the Church.

— *C. Donald Cole*

Introduction

A Greek professor, early in my seminary career at Dallas Theological Seminary, first piqued my interest about a group of Christians in England who created a movement which impacted all of Christendom throughout the United Kingdom. I can vividly recall this professor's description of these church leaders who came together in the 1830s and 1840s and committed themselves to following New Testament principles for the church, whatever this might cost them. At the time, I knew I wanted to know more about that group and the principles that created such a renewal.

So it has been that for the past 25 years I have studied them and admired them and discussed their work with others. I now know a great deal about that group of Christians and the principles they rediscovered that gave rise to the original Brethren renewal. There is no question that it was a genuine renewal. The Spirit of God was obviously at work. Biblical truth that had been neglected and almost forgotten was recaptured with a spirit that was contagious. Truth concerning the unity of the Body of Christ, the centrality of worship and the priesthood of all believers began to take on meaning that was equivalent to the joy of new birth. With the Scriptures as their source and the Holy Spirit as their guide, a small band of committed Anglican scholars became, in a spontaneous way, the architects of what is known as the Plymouth Brethren movement. Even those who were critical of the renewal were impressed by its impact. At the turn of this century, William Neatby wrote of them:

> The Brethren sought to effect a fresh start without authority, precedent or guidance beyond the letter of Holy Scripture. For them, essentially, the garnered experience of 18 centuries was as though it were not. Such an experiment in the hands of eminent men could scarcely fail to yield a considerable harvest of interest and instruction (1901:3).

The harvest of interest and instruction was impressive. Scarcely a town or village in all of England was untouched by the renewal. In spite of some divisions and doctrinal distortions, the renewal movement continued to grow and spread, moving to Ireland and Scotland. By 1870 the Brethren had crossed the Atlantic and started to spread throughout North America. Today we find there are about 1200 Brethren congregations throughout the United States and Canada.

My wife, Ann, was raised in one of these congregations and she has been involved with them virtually all her life. I became enamored with the Brethren while a graduate student. The simplicity of the church in the New Testament with its powerful and all inclusive priciples soon caused me to seek out those who believed that those principles could be practiced today. We found such a group and we have been with them ever since. Being thoroughly convinced of the New Testament position on the church we became part of the Brethren family. Just as it is necessary to understand the dynamics that have made our own family become what it is, it is also necessary for me to understand the dynamics that have made my church become what it is. In doing this I am really understanding myself since I am an extension of that family.

One thing has come clear to me in doing this study: nothing remains static. Families grow and change as children reach maturity, the elders die off, and new members are added through marriage and birth. So churches are never static because there are new dynamics to contend with.

Further, the universal church of Jesus Christ has always been in the process of renewal. Sometimes this takes the form of a revival within a particular group while other times renewal is a reformation with a definite separation from the former tradition. Church history demonstrates that this process is cyclical in nature— with periods of decline followed by an outpouring of God's Spirit. A corporate declension of the church occurs because of the natural inclination towards sin within all believers. There is a seducing tendency for faith to be pulled toward a rigid and formal religion— which is then pulled, eventually, to open secularity and on to apostasy. Fortunately, God, in his providence, enters this cycle and breathes new life into his people. Where new wine is made, the old forms and structures simply yield. The life of God cannot be suppressed, it must be expressed.

So I became a product of a renewing process which came to be known throughout the world as the Plymouth Brethren movement, called the Christian Brethren or the Brethren.

In my fascination with the history of my tradition, I undertook the study which results in this book. This study also springs from a deep-seated longing for renewal among those known as Plymouth Brethren—the church I have served for 22 years. As a young seminary student, I became convinced of the New Testament church principles which I see are the keys to continuing growth and renewal.

During these 22 years of service my early idealism has given way to realism without, I hope, too much pessimism. Unfortunately, I have seen many committed servants among the Plymouth Brethren become disillusioned during this period. Too often disillusionment turns to cynicism. I made a convenant with God not to let that happen to me, but in going through this process of idealism to realism, I have learned a great deal. God has taught me through my reading and exposure to other Christians that he often blesses people I disagree with and he doesn't bother to ask for my permission.

I have learned there is a difference between having a good sermon outline and a real message from God. I have learned that how one holds one's convictions is often more important than the convictions themselves. I have learned to clarify in my own mind the difference between the essentials of faith and the nonessentials without compromising Scripture. I have learned not to be threatened by truth because all truth is God's truth. I have learned when I meet other Christians to major on those things on which we agree and to let our disagreements go. I have learned not to be enamored by the latest trend in Christian circles.

I am not interested in change without understanding the purpose of change. I am not interested in the secrets of the Christian life but in living the Christian life. What I am interested in is being like David and serving my generation in the will of God (Ac 13:36). I want to keep growing, even though I find it more difficult the older I become to change. Change involves challenge and we all need challenges that will cause us to dig deeper into the Scriptures and to lay hold of the unshakable foundation of our faith.

My spiritual pilgrimage thus brought me to this study of renewal and its history in the Brethren. It also brought me to making statistical studies, accompanied by an analytical inductive survey, to discover what has happened to the renewal movement that created the Plymouth Brethren assemblies in the first place. The question I needed to answer was why the Brethren in the United States are declining so rapidly. I began to ask certain questions of those I met who had left the Brethren. Finally, I made a more formal study and interviewed not only the disenchanted I discovered but also current leaders in the assemblies.

To assess these answers and my findings I felt it was necessary to set forth my understanding of a biblical doctrine of the church. This is a synthesis of my understanding of the nature and function of the church and is the basis for the proposals and strategies I set forth for renewal today.

Because, even though, what I would wish for the Brethren today is a dynamic renewal movement, before strategies and proposals can be suggested, one must have an understanding of the dynamics that have caused the decline of the Plymouth Brethren assemblies. That understanding cannot be gained apart from having some historical knowledge of the original Plymouth Brethren movement. Those early Brethren rediscovered biblical principles of the church and they enjoyed phenomenal success and growth.

Unfortunately, the biblical principles that were rediscovered began to be interpreted in a narrow way without any flex at all. This, coupled with the influence of the most powerful leader in the movement, served to introduce a definite distortion into the original vision of the Brethren. These distortions have influenced the Brethren even to this day.

Regaining the original vision of the Brethren and rediscovery of biblical principles which created the movement is an imperative for the Brethren today if we are not going to decline into oblivion. So this study puts forth an analysis of the early understanding of the Brethren with modern applications of these biblical methods for renewal today. By evaluating the local assembly we posit some conclusions that lead us to make some specific strategies which we trust will be helpful to all who look for renewal—within and without the Brethren church.

Finally, we need to say that the overriding intent of this study is the hope and prayer that God would breathe new life into the Plymouth Brethren assemblies. Apart from this, anything said would be nothing more than a voice in the wilderness.

Roots of the Brethren Renewal

1

In order to evaluate the motivating factors that created so much success in the original Brethren renewal, one must look beyond the historical conditions of the established church or dissenting churches to deduce the reasons for the Brethren renewal. A spiritual reality is hard to objectify.

The method chosen here to evaluate the success of the early Brethren is based upon Paul S. Minear's thesis found in his *Images of the Church in the New Testament.* He posits that to understand the New Testament church one must understand the images used to describe the church in the New Testament. Since the church is essentially a mystery (Ep 3:4-6), it becomes difficult to perceive its nature apart from metaphorical language. The church is a living organism which is a spiritual reality. In order to understand the nature and purpose of its reality, one needs their imagination awakened—which is precisely what images do. Where images describe life, doctrines describe structure.

The New Testament church contains 95 identifiable images of the church. The original Brethren renewal was also an alive and vibrant movement that is best described in terms of the life that the early Brethren were experiencing rather than the doctrine that subsequently came from the movement. This life can also be related to the New Testament images of the church, for the original Brethren recaptured the imagination and vitality of some of those images.

It is important to note that images also help advance self-understanding. This is true not only of individuals but also of groups and movements. As individuals, every person carries a series of self-images. How that person integrates those images will determine, to a large extent, their success. This was also a factor in the original Brethren movement. The community had an image of itself that played an important part in its success. Minear points out how vital this corporate image was:

> Its self-understanding, its inner cohesion, its esprit de corps, derive from a dominant image of itself, even though that image remains inarticulately embedded in the subconscious strata. If an inauthentic image dominates its consciousness, there will first be signs of malaise, followed by more overt tokens of communal deterioration. If an authentic image is recognized at the verbal level but denied in practice, there will also follow sure disintegration of the ligaments of corporate life. The process of discovering and rediscovering an authentic self-image will involve the whole community, not only in clear-headed conceptual thinking and disciplined speech, but also in a rebirth of its images and its imaginations, and in the absorption of these images into the interstices of communal activities of every sort (1960:24).

The original Brethren experienced this rebirth of biblical images, and this was inarticulately embedded deeply in the corporate subconscious of the renewal movement. So they were feeling and . experiencing the life of God in the rediscovering of what it meant to be the church of God, even though they could not articulate precisely what this was. The three groups— in Dublin, Plymouth and Bristol— were discovering what it meant to let the church be the church.

The Church as the Temple of God

The metaphor of the church being the temple of God implies, first of all, that the church is to be a worshiping community (1 P 2: 4-5). The early Brethren, in a dramatic way, recaptured this truth. In the New Testament the body of the individual believer is pictured as being a temple of God (1 Co 6:19) but the individual Christian is also pictured as being a member of a local temple which is the local church (1 Co 3:16-17). These two metaphors underscore both the individual and corporate importance of worship— a truth captured by the original Brethren from Plymouth, Dublin and Bristol who were known for their personal piety as well as their corporate worship.

Probably the most attractive element the original Brethren displayed to the age in which they lived was their personal devotion to Jesus Christ. Worship must always remain the foremost priority for the believer, and the early Brethren captured the greatest command, "You shall love the Lord your God with all your heart, and with all your soul, and with all your mind" with their commitment to the Lordship of Christ. Although these Brethren had many critics who could not accept their teaching or practice, none of them denied the force of their personal piety or the fact that they were people who took seriously their personal worship by living lives of simplicity and godliness.

Another important element of worship in both the New and Old Testaments is the idea of sacrifice. This, too, was part of early Brethren experience, for they were known for their sacrificial lifestyle which became embedded in the soul of the Brethren renewal movement. This level of exceptional personal piety sparked life and awakened many imaginations as to what the church was all about.

Interestingly, many of the early leaders came from nobility and wealth. John Darby not only came from a wealthy family, but he got his middle name, Nelson, from his godfather, Lord Nelson, the naval hero who died at the Battle of Trafalgar in 1805. Although Darby's father was a wealthy landowner and merchant, because of his deep devotion to Christ, he turned his back on his family's wealth, and his father disinherited him when he refused to pursue a legal career. John Darby also sacrificed marriage and a family so he could serve God more fully. At one point, engaged to Lady Theodosia Powerscourt, he broke off the engagement because she, in his view, did not share his depth of commitment to the ministry.

Early in the movement the idea of "meeting in the name of Jesus only" was applied to corporate worship as a statement against the sectarian spirit that was strangling the dissenting churches. Denominational blinders were preventing many believers from worshiping with anyone except those who subscribed to their own group's doctrinal beliefs.

With the Brethren, the communion service began to be seen as a symbol of unity, especially in Plymouth where the Monday evening Bible lectures became a place that the Lord's Supper was introduced as a symbol of unity. Clergy from the national church and dissenting churches joined with the Brethren from Plymouth in a format that permitted all to read, speak, pray or lead a hymn. It is interesting to note that there is evidence that early in the renewal at Plymouth, women participated verbally in the meetings (Coad 1966:66).

Anthony Norris Groves, a great proponent for unity in the renewal movement, stressed that corporate worship was to be based upon one's common life in Christ. No one, according to Groves, should be rejected from corporate worship just because they belonged to the established church or to a dissenting church. Life in Jesus Christ was more important than any particular denominational distinctive. Since worship is based on life and love, it must transcend doctrine and opinion. No conditions ought to be placed on worship other than the conditions for salvation.

Such ideas were revolutionary in those days, yet they caught the imagination of those believers who longed to express their oneness in a religious world that was structured to deny such oneness. The principle of inclusive unity with diversity practically expressed in worship around the one loaf and one cup as the one Body of Christ was beautiful and biblical. The early Brethren recaptured an almost lost and forgotten truth.

The Church as the Household of God

Another image the original Brethren recaptured for us was found in the metaphor of the church as the household of God (1 Tm 3:15; Ep 2:19; Heb 2:6). This image conveys the profound concept of the church as family whose principal characteristic is to be loved and accepted.

The original Brethren from Plymouth, Dublin and Bristol worked at practicing family. Many of the early leadership had trained for the Anglican clergy. Not only were they well educated, but they also came from the upper stratum of that society. These early Brethren saw the truth of being the household of God to all believers and worked hard at expressing acceptance and love for those who were poor and uneducated. It was common for wealthy Brethren to treat their Christian servants as family, and stories are told of servants eating at the same table with their employers— a rarity in that society.

Also, deliberate attempts were made by the wealthy to live simple life-styles. For instance, since floor carpets were a conspicuous evidence of wealth, often early Brethren displayed bare floors. Many of the early wealthy Brethren lived in modest homes.

Some leaders found it difficult to adjust to a simple life-style and advantages and disassociate themselves from the pleasures that came with nobility.

Still the Brethren took seriously the concept of family equality, and some made deliberate attempts at practicing communal living. Although the early Brethren never formed a separate Christian community in which everyone had everything in common, they did practice a form of semicommunal living. They visited freely in each other's homes and met frequently for meals and fellowship. In those early days they became known as those who forsook all things and showed hospitality to all people. This latter characteristic is still true to a great extent, for the Brethren are known to be people given to hospitality.

This desire to show love and acceptance to the uneducated and the poor was well illustrated in the life of John Nelson Darby who obviously preferred being with the poor. He first became a successful curate in the Anglican church because of his work with poor Irish peasants. Although Darby was theologically trained to be a scholar and could easily hold his own with intellectuals, still his real love in ministry was with the poor and ignorant. Stories abound about his ministry to the poor. On one occasion he took the place of a poor believer who was sick and labored for over a week doing his menial work so he would not lose his job. When Darby traveled, he deliberately refused to stay with the average or well-off Christian but instead would stay with the poorer believers.

One reason that Darby deliberately did this came from his own uneasiness over so many from the Anglican nobility who were leaving the established church to join the Brethren movement. In fact, often the fashionable and well-educated people who wanted to leave the Anglican church, because they regarded it as corrupt and dead, found it easier to adjust to the Brethren movement than the other older forms of dissent which had a reputation for vulgarity and radicalism (Rowdon 1967:276).

Apparently the intellectual integrity and the genuine spiritual life displayed by the Brethren in their concern for the poor caused many in the Anglican church to join them. Also the principle of inclusive unity with diversity meant they could find a high degree of tolerance and acceptance in this group.

Anthony Norris Groves, better than any other of the early Brethren, captured the true ecumenical spirit behind the meaning of the image of the household of God when he wrote:

1. The basis of our fellowship is LIFE in the Christ of Scripture rather than LIGHT on the teaching of the Scriptures. Those who have part with Christ have part with us. Because our communion is one of life and love more than one of doctrine and opinion, we seek to show that the oneness in the life of God through Jesus Christ is a stronger bond than that of being one of us— whether organizationally or denominationally.

2. Because our fellowship is based on our common life in Christ, we do not reject anyone because of the organization or denomination with which they may be affiliated; nor would we hold them responsible for the conduct within that system, any more than we would a child for the conduct in the home of which they are merely a part.

3. We do not feel it desirable to withdraw from fellowship with any Christians except at the point where they may require us to do what our consciences will not permit, or restrain us from doing what our consciences require. Even then, we maintain our fellowship with them in any matter where we are not called upon to so compromise. This ensures that (insofar as we understand the Scripture) we do not separate ourselves from them any further than they separate themselves from Christ.

4. We do not consider an act of fellowship to be indicative of total agreement; indeed we sometimes find it a needed expression of love to submit to others in matters where we do not fully agree, rather than to prevent some greater good from being brought about. Our choice would be to bear with their wrong rather than separate ourselves from their good.

5. We believe it more scriptural to reflect a heart of love, ready to find a covering for faults, than to constantly look for that with which we may disagree. We will then be known more by what we witness *for* than by what we witness *against.*

6. We feel it biblical never to pressure anyone to *act* in uniformity farther than they *feel* in uniformity; we use our fellowship in the Spirit as an opportunity to discuss our differences and find this to be the most effective way of leading others— or being led by them— into the light of the Word.

7. While enjoying such a wide range of Christian fellowship, we would not force this liberty upon those who feel otherwise minded. In such circumstances, we enjoy fellowship as far as *they* will permit, then pray that the Lord would lead them further into this true liberty of the common life in Christ (n.d.:1-2).

This beautifully articulated truth of what it means to be family is as applicable today as it was when it was written, because it is deeply embedded in the Word of God and in the life the church. Truly the early Brethren recaptured the life of worship and the meaning of being family.

The Church as the People of God

In the process of letting the church be the church, the Brethren were experiencing what it meant to be the people of God. The image of the church as the people of God contains many metaphors that revolve around that concept. The overriding truth conveyed, however, is that the church as the people of God is to be a witness in the world (1 P 2:9-10) and this helps to give meaning to the concept of being saints. The meaning behind the title saint is this: the believer is to be set apart so that they might be different from others in their service to God. The church as the people of God, therefore, means to bear the title of saint and to be a different people while serving God in the world. Certainly this was true of the early Brethren who were different in their life-style and also were a witness, impacting the world in which they lived.

George Muller is a good example of this, for he made an impact not only in Bristol but around the world. Muller, motivated by the gospel of love and concern, saw a crying social problem that needed to be addressed. The black plague that had struck England had left orphans and destitute children throughout the country. Muller began taking the children in off the streets to provide them break-fast. While they ate he would read the Scriptures to them. This practice gradually led to his founding first a day school and then eventually an orphanage. This orphanage grew enormously until there were five main dormitories called Ashley Downs.

When George Muller died, over 10,000 orphans had passed through Ashley Downs, three million dollars had been spent on them and 114,000 children had gone through the day school and breakfast programs. This astonishing program had been accom-plished by Muller without his making any pleas for money. Not only this, but Muller was the financial mainstay for Brethren missionary work around the world, and over a million dollars had been sent to support missions through his orphanage. Obviously, George Muller was a person who saw a need and did something about it.

Though Muller and his work were exceptional in scope, they were not exceptional in practice. As a rule, the early Brethren saw themselves as bearing witness that they were the people of God when they became involved in meeting real needs. For example, Thomas Barnardo began to feed hungry and homeless boys in London. Eventually, this project grew into a huge institution for homeless children, and some feel this work eclipsed Muller's, even though it never got the same kind of public exposure. J. W. C. Fegan was another concerned for the poor children and for alcoholics. His concern and efforts on their behalf were so impressive that even the Charles Darwin family supported him (Coad 1966:179).

Robert Chapman, from the Barnstable area of England, left a prominent legal profession to minister among the poor. He became well-known as an evangelist but what gave credibility to the gospel he preached was his deep concern for poor people. One appreciative person wrote a letter of gratitude to Chapman, not knowing his address. Interestingly, Chapman received it addressed simply to "R. C. Chapman, University of Love, England" (ibid:72).

But not all the original Brethren leaders were well-educated nobility. Robert Gribble was an uneducated, middle-class person who took seriously his witness, working with the poor and downtrodden and becoming one of the leading evangelists in the early days of the movement. It was reported that John Darby once asked G. V. Wigram, "How is it, Wigram, that although you and I preach the gospel more clearly than many, we see so few results, yet they tell us that in North Devon, this Mr. Gribble, in his meetings, repeats only a few gospel texts and makes a few simple remarks and souls are saved and assemblies formed?" (Rowdon 1967:152-153).

This drive to witness and be the people of God caused the early Brethren to be one of the most aggressive of all the Protestant traditions in missions. Church historian, Kenneth Scott Latourette, claims that the Plymouth Brethren missionaries were among the finest in Guatemala, Honduras, Venezuela, India and Indochina around the turn of this century (1970:312-313, 321, 409, 424).

Many examples could be cited showing how the early Brethren were a different people in the world who were committed to being the people of God. Consequently, this meant for them making a serious attempt to meet the needs of the poor, the distressed and the destitute. This is consistent with church history, for as one scholar notes:

Renewal in the church has usually meant the church's rebirth among the poor, the masses, the alienated. And with such resurgence has usually come the recovery of such essential New Testament emphases as community, purity, discipleship, the priesthood of believers and the gifts of the Spirit (Snyder 1975:51).

The early Brethren were experiencing this resurgence of life and a recovery of truth, grasping the essence of what Jesus meant in the parable of the Good Samaritan: If you love God, you will love your neighbor, and if you love God, you will know who your neighbor is. Your neighbor is anyone whose need you see and whose need you can meet (Lk 10:25-37).

The early Brethren devotedly loved God, not just because they worshiped the Lord regularly at the Lord's Supper nor because they preached the gospel throughout England and Ireland, but because they identified their neighbors and reached out to meet them in their need. This gave the gospel they preached credibility, and they learned the secret of the Christian witness and what it means to be the people of God in their generation—Christian presence must accompany gospel preaching.

The Church as the Body of Christ

The image of the church as the Body of Christ is the most complicated metaphor used of the church. However unique it may be, it nonetheless suggests that the church should be understood primarily as an organic reality rather than an institutional structure. The practical importance of this is that in function the Body of Christ is interdependent. Since it is composed of many parts which are related to each other, all are necessary for normal and healthy function. In the body metaphor, the individual parts function through spiritual gifts. These two main ideas—the church seen as an organism and the church functioning through spiritual gifts—were emphasized by the early Brethren.

The Brethren stressed the church as an organic reality in contrast to viewing it as an institution. Many people in those days perceived the established church as having grown cold, formal and dead and felt it was difficult to find evidence of genuine life there. Darby made this admission:

> It was not the details of the sacramental and priestly system which drove me from the establishment, deadly as they are in their nature.

It was that I was looking for the *Body of Christ*. It was not there, but in all the parish perhaps not one converted person. . . (n.d.:445).

Darby found the Body of Christ he was looking for in the life, worship, community and people of Plymouth, Dublin and Bristol who were committed to being the Body of Christ.

Reacting Against the Establishment

2

Not only was it the lack of life in the established church that the early Brethren reacted strongly against, they also were put off by the institutional structure of the church which they accused of stifling what little life might exist there. The Body of Christ, in their opinion, was not free to serve or worship in an institution that permitted only clergy to exercise their gifts. Before one could fully serve the church, they had to be ordained. Before one could fully lead in worship, one had to be ordained. In searching Scriptures, the early Brethren found that the established church's concept of ordination was an institutional truth, not a biblical one.

Anthony Norris Groves is a good example of this conflict. Although motivated by love for God and wanting to be free to worship and serve God, yet he, on every hand, was thwarted from this. Finally, he opted for God's freedom and decided he would worship without restriction and serve without restraint along with any others in the Body of Christ who also met simply in the name of the Lord Jesus. Since there was only one body, all names and titles were derived from the institutional concept of the church and not from the Scriptures. This stance for Groves went both ways, and he would not separate himself personally from any believer because of their titles or identifying names.

Even though they demonstrated such tolerance, the early Brethren were perceived at almost every point as being in conflict with the institutional church. They were noncreedal, taking as their only creed the Word of God, while the institutional church was based upon a creedal declaration.

The early Brethren practiced believer baptism,* whereas they saw the institutional church as indiscriminately baptizing everyone without regard to age and faith. They saw the institutional church practicing indiscriminate communion to anyone who had membership in the church, regardless of whether or not they demonstrated a life in Christ. The Brethren, however, broke bread with those who did so in the name of Jesus, implying that they had a believing faith.

So the Brethren saw the established church as possessing little life in comparison to their own exuberant vitality, and in their view the Anglican church had lost its life and purity. They felt there was no alternative but to separate and identify with life, the organic Body of Christ.

The obvious question is why these early Brethren did not identify with the dissenting churches. They were certainly part of the Body of Christ, and no one would deny they had life. They were pure churches in that their membership was limited to genuine believers. But the early Brethren were not attracted to these groups because it would have violated the one Body of Christ image. They saw their renewal as a unity movement. The very existence of so many different dissenting churches denied the unity of the Body of Christ while sectarian names such as Baptist, Congregationalist, Presbyterian and Wesleyan simply promoted the shameful condition of disunity. The early Brethren felt compelled to build the Body of Christ on the dual theme of unity and purity, allowing their spiritual gifts to be exercised. The three major biblical passages which discuss spiritual gifts do so within the metaphor of the Body of Christ (Rm 12; 1 Co 12-14; Ep 4). Also, the larger context in each of these passages deals with the subject of unity.

Reclaiming the almost forgotten truths regarding the spiritual gifts and the functional priesthood of all believers proved to play a vital role in the Brethren movement. Freedom to worship and to serve and to exercise one's gifts freely are cardinal truths among Brethren.

The early Brethren faced some interesting problems that focused around spiritual gifts. Those at Plymouth, and later at the other centers of Brethren renewal, flirted for a time with the so-called charis-

---

*Although a percentage of the early Brethren continued to practice infant and household baptism.

matic gifts (supernatural gifts). In fact, some critics of the Brethren renewal have tried to link the origins of the Brethren to a little-known charismatic phenomenon that occurred at about the same time (MacPherson 1975). The truth, however, is that the early Brethren did take this charismatic phenomenon seriously but subsequently concluded—after much examination—to reject the experience as an aberration from the normal workings of the Spirit of God.

Another problem that confronted the early Brethren in the free use of spiritual gifts was control—particularly at the Lord's Supper. In the early days because large numbers were being converted through evangelistic efforts, many ignorant and illiterate people were participating at the open worship service. Also, the platform ministry was affected because many zealous but ignorant believers wanted to preach.

Finally at Plymouth, through Darby's influence, controls were placed on both the Lord's Supper and the platform (Coad 1966:63). A presiding elder was chosen to maintain order and to restrain any plainly unprofitable participants. Gradually the Brethren moved away from this control toward a more open communion to what has been called impulsive leading and ministry.

Interestingly enough, the early Brethren never did achieve uniformity with regard to the breaking of bread meeting. Some retained a presiding elder idea and others prearranged the order by having designated people give thanks for the bread and cup, while yet others went to a completely open format. In spite of these two minor problems, the early Brethren successfully reclaimed the almost forgotten truth that every believer has a spiritual gift and everyone has a place of service.

The Spirit of God in a unique way was working in England and Ireland in the 1820s and 1830s. The cycle of renewal was in process. The Anglican church had drifted from formalism to secularity and was sliding towards what some regarded as apostasy. Christians began to respond to God's Word. Life began to awaken spontaneously in the hearts of many and the Body of Christ began to express itself in new ways.

New forms of worship began to emerge as the truths of the priesthood of all believers took on new meaning. Freedom to serve God through exercising the gifts of the Spirit and the freedom to worship led the Brethren to meet real and felt needs in their world. The poor and the destitute were taken seriously and the people of

God began doing the work of God. Their caring made an impact for God that awakened the conscience of others.

Thousands of other Christians began to witness the Body of Christ alive and active in the world, and the Brethren were like a magnet to those longing for spiritual reality. Many turned to the Lord as the gospel was preached by those who had the integrity of committed lives behind them.

The Historical Context

3

The original Brethren would have said that a brief survey of their history must begin with the Word of God. This is true because the founding Brethren were deeply committed to God's Word and the Scriptures became their constitution, guiding them to renewal. "It has no parallel in the whole history of the church of God because in no other instance has the Word of God (freed from tradition) been taken as the guide of those who have sought a revival in the church of God" (Soltau 1863:6-7). This might appear a bold and exaggerated statement in view of the whole scope of church history; however, for one who lived through the early days of Brethren expansion, such enthusiasm can be understood. There were, however, spiritual and historical antecedents to this movement.

Church historians agree that the famous prereformation philosopher from Oxford, John Wyclif (1329-1384), was a prominent person in English church history. Today he is remembered for his early translation of the Bible into English; however, his greatest contribution to church history in general and to the Brethren movement in particular came from his theological thinking. As a Roman Catholic academician, he was considered to be a radical and later judged a heretic by the church. In fact, 40 years after his death, the Roman church dug up his bones, tried him as a heretic and burned his remains at the stake. But what was poison to Rome became the seed doctrines of the great reformation and the underlying issues of the Brethren renewal of 1820-1830. This prophetic forerunner, predating the Brethren movement by 500 years, operated out of Oxford University—and Oxford later was at the heart of the Brethren movement.

By redefining the nature of the church, Wyclif rejected the Roman position that the church was an organized body composed of those in the Roman church who had received the sacraments (baptism, confirmation, communion, etc.). This church was a visible identity of the Kingdom of God. Wyclif, looking to the New Testament for his definition of church, concluded that it was rather the body of the elect—therefore an invisible unity rather than a visible identity. (This particular concept became a real point of contention later in the history of the Brethren.) Wyclif went further in his thinking stating the true church did not need any priest acting as a mediator between people and God other than Jesus Christ. In fact, there are no clergy in the true church because all are priests before God (another parallel with the later Brethren renewal).

Wyclif posited Scriptures as the overall authority, not the church—becoming the forerunner not only of the Reformation battle cry, "Sola Scriptura" (sole sufficiency of the Scriptures), but also of the early Brethren who saw their renewal effort deeply rooted in the Word of God (and who became known popularly as "People of the Book").

The Roman Catholic teaching on the eucharist (communion) was particularly offensive to Wyclif who rejected the idea that the bread and wine were literally transformed into the body and blood of Jesus (transubstantiation). This he called idolatry. The early Brethren, also, always emphasized the eucharist, with some suggesting that Brethren theology can be understood only as a "eucharistic theology or eucharistic polity" (McLaren 1976:314). Another church historian has said:

> In the history of movements of spiritual renewal, however, as well as in common observation of parishioners, it is apparent that where the truths embodied in the Lord's Supper are clearly taught and proclaimed, spiritual renewal is present, but where the sacraments are administered without much explanation simply as a kind of medicine, a palpable deadness may set in (Lovelace 1980:170).

Thus John Wyclif in an amazing way was a prophetic forerunner of the early Brethren.

Thomas Cranmer (1489-1556), the Archbishop of Canterbury under Henry VIII, led England out of Catholicism during the Reformation and then became the chief architect of the Church of England under King Edward VI. The cycle soon began to move the church toward the seducing tendency of a rigid and formal religion which began to dominate. Soon God allowed a new wine to brew in the established church and three distinct renewal movements began in the Anglican church prior to the Brethren renewal.

The Puritans derived their name from their stated mission of wanting to purify the Church of England of its "popish and Romish trappings." They attempted and briefly succeeded in overthrowing the monarchy, but failed in establishing a Puritan church. On Oliver Cromwell's death, the monarchy was reestablished and the Anglican church was again in control. This church has always struggled with extremes— on one hand being pulled toward Romanism and on the other toward Puritanism. King James I (who gave us the King James Bible) was firmly anti-Puritan. The persecution of this group caused a small percentage of them to leave England, sailing for America, where they hoped to find religious freedom. Others left the "polluted and false" Anglican church forming churches which became known first as Independent congregations, then later as Congregationalists and Independent Baptists (the issue of baptism separating the two).

Another movement which was not an attempt at reform within the established church, as the Puritan movement had been, was the Quaker movement— more properly known as the Society of Friends. This separatist movement was founded by George Fox, who had a vision of Christ gathering people into a victory over Satan. He preached to the Anglicans about the corruptness of their church and many did separate and establish the Society of Friends. Their distinctive characteristic has been their emphasis upon the Spirit's leading— which strongly influenced the Brethren movement, some feel (Stunt 1970).

Then a hundred years before the Brethren renewal began, the Anglican church experienced revival. In 1729 at Oxford University a group of Anglican students met to further their devotion to God. Called the "Holy Club of Oxford," they were led by John and Charles Wesley who had been profoundly influenced by European pietism. Their stated objective was to provide a disciplined method of spiritual improvement. Each evening, John and Charles Wesley and a number of others committed themselves to prayer and Bible study. Because of their emphasis upon a method of discipline, they were labeled "Methodist"— and here began the great Methodist revival. This was not a separatist movement for there was never any intention of forming a new tradition. In fact, John Wesley never left the church and died an Anglican in 1791. Not until 1795 did Methodism finally secede from the established church.

This revival was a remarkable work of God where thousands were converted. Wesley formed societies essentially to disciple the large number of converts. These grew larger and larger and soon became a national organization with a set of rules and disciplines, leaders chosen and lay preachers were appointed. Assistants were ordained by Wesley to administer the sacraments— all without the permission of the Anglican church who took offense as the line separating clergy and laity was broken down. The influence of all this on the Brethren movement— which would follow some 35 years after the Methodist church was founded— is undeniable.

The effects of the Wesleyan revival were nothing short of incredible. English culture and the Church of England never were the same again. Influential Anglicans were converted who in turn took their faith into their spheres. Members of Parliament sat under the preaching of John Wesley and one— William Wilberforce— joined with a group of committed Christians to pass legislature that stopped slavery in the United Kingdom in 1807. They also initiated penal, parliamentary, and child labor reforms and helped open India up for the mission begun by William Carey. These committed Christians were dedicated to the Kingdom of God and to their world, England.

Unfortunately, the Wesleyans who separated from the church, forming the Methodist denomination, developed a form of pietism that led to grim legalism and sectarianism. Their catechism for the Assistants in the Society instructs firmly:

Q   What are the rules of an Assistant?

A   1. Be diligent. Never be unemployed a moment, never be triflingly employed, never while away time; spend no more time at any place than is strictly necessary.

2. Be serious. Let your motto be, "holiness unto the Lord." Avoid all lightness as you would avoid hell-fire, and laughing as you would cursing and swearing (Coad 1968:262).

Schools for the children of Wesley's workers were founded and designed to regiment the children's lives so it would have been virtually impossible to keep all the rules and regulations. Children were even forbade from playing, rather they must be holy and serious at all times (loc cit). This legalistic piety, although never to this extreme, had its effects on the early Brethren.

These three movements— the Puritans, the Quakers, and the Wesleyans— were examples of how the Spirit of God was working through His people to restore life and vitality in the church. All three renewal movements laid important groundwork for the Brethren renewal— about to burst on the scene in Ireland and England.

At the beginning of the 19th Century, the world was in transition. The French Revolution had ended by 1795 but its effects were still being felt. Although Wellington defeated Napoleon at Waterloo, Europe was still in turmoil. Nationalism and democracy were emerging, along with nationalistic deism. In England the Parliament was facing unrest and disorder. Reform was needed.

Economically, the industrial revolution had come to England— heretofore primarily a rural economy. Becoming an urban society caused major changes in population distribution as people moved to the cities. Soon England was labeled as the "workshop of the world" as the estimated population in the British Isles increased from ten million to over 30 million during the industrial revolution (McDowell 1963:12).

The Anglican church was in sad condition during the decade, 1820-30. A bishop within the established church charged that the clergy were in a shameful condition and not since the time of the Wesleyan revivals had the church faced such a deplorable situation. One critic of the state church described it as a "machine of the Antichrist" and hoped that an Act of Parliament would abolish its privileged status, putting it on an equal footing with the other Christian sects (Rowdon 1967:3).

Parliamentary reform was seen as a terrible threat to the clergy, for while Parliament was trying to make itself more representative of the people, the clergy were trying to maintain the status quo. They were fearful of the rising power of the irreligious lower class, and with no separation of church and state, political reform was seen as a secularizing compromise which could alter their favored status of that society. The popular critics of the day accused the clergy of being corrupt and deficient in their religious duties because they spent too much time becoming wealthy in business affairs. Some were even accused of running four or five businesses alongside their religious duties— which suffered as a result. Clerics were accused of preaching lifeless and boring sermons because showing enthusiasm in a sermon was grounds for being charged a Methodist. One Anglican vicar was accused of being a "nonconformist" because he led his congregation in the singing of Psalms and hymns he had compiled and resorted to extemporary preaching (ibid:4).

While these popular grievances were generating a lot of heat, behind the scenes an important ecclesiastical development was taking place at Oxford University. This became known as the Oxford movement or sometimes called the Tractarian Revival.* This movement was a student revolt against the general conditions of the established church and an academic backlash toward the existing problems in the church. It was to have considerable import on the Brethren renewal movement. The principal leader in the Oxford movement was John Henry Newman who was concerned about the condition of the church, yet he saw Parliamentary reform as a great threat to the church. Since non-Anglicans and even the irreligious could be members of Parliament, scholars like Newman who perceived the biblical criticism rising in Germany as undermining biblical authority, began to place more faith in the church as the ultimate authority. Newman gradually came to believe that the only way to renew the Anglican church was to return to the only true church, Rome. Although he failed in his attempt, he eventually converted to Catholicism and died a famous cardinal. Interestingly, his brother, Francis had the exact opposite reaction. He also sought renewal, but sided with the Brethren effort. These two brothers, both evangelical Christians, yet took two different pilgrimages. Francis moved through Anglicanism into the Brethren renewal, then later into the Unitarian movement and finally into agnosticism.

The generic term "dissenting churches" is used of all the Protestant groups dissenting from the state church—including the Methodists, the Baptists, the Congregationalists, the Quakers and the Presbyterians. Some of these churches were originally independent, but usually they drifted in time into one of the identifiable dissenting groups.

All these dissenting churches played an important part in continuing the spirit of the Wesleyan revival, for genuine spiritual vigor existed in these churches. Some groups realized they needed to be flexible to reach the masses— whose lives were controlled by the new forces of the industrial revolution— so arranged their church services to meet the needs of the common people. Preaching services were even sometimes held in the coal mines or in town halls— in stark contrast to the formal structured approach of the Anglican church— which finally tried to counter the success of the dissenting churches by establishing chapels in the poorer neighborhoods. These chapels became not only preaching stations but, in

---

* Because of the large number of tracts that were written and circulated.

places, also a sort of all-purpose relief headquarters for needy people in the neighborhood. Eventually, the chapels were seen as counterproductive to the established church because they began to align themselves with the dissenting churches.

These were difficult times for those in the dissenting churches. England was still a church-state, and those not in the church suffered discrimination. If you belonged to a dissenting church, it was difficult to get a marriage license, because they were issued through the state church system. This was equally true for funerals and political activities. Education was a particular problem because all the universities were run by the Anglican church. Finally, a society was formed to protect the religious freedom of all Protestant groups.

The situation of the dissenting churches created internal tension for evangelicals within the Anglican church who could neither deny the validity of the faith walk of those in the dissenting churches, nor the corruptness of the Anglican church. Yet, their strong convictions on the unity of the Body of Christ meant that the established church had to be, in their minds, the only true visible expression of Christ's body. Ipso facto, those leaving the church were sectarian and were creating schisms.

The dissenting churches, however, were not without their own problems. Although separated from the "corrupt church" to found the "pure church," they began to separate again from each other. Soon there was a variety of different Methodists, Baptists and independents—and most of these groups would have little to do with each other. Each group tended to a sectarian attitude toward all others who called themselves Christian, refusing to fellowship with any outside their own group. Their names became sectarian labels that kept them from recognizing any form of unity.

Soon you had a situation in which the established church had unity (at least from their own perspective) but did not have purity. On the other hand, the dissenting churches had purity (from their viewpoint), but they did not have unity. They claimed to be the true church because they were pure, yet the by-products of their stance were division and a sectarian attitude. The established church, for its part, claimed to be the true church because of its unity, accusing all the others of creating schisms. The by-products of its unity were cold theology and corruption.

The Search for Unity and Purity

4

Within both the established church and the dissenting church existed voices crying for unity. Some Anglican leaders pleaded with the dissenters to return to their church and work for renewal. A prominent dissenting church leader deplored the exclusive tendencies and sectarian attitude he found in his church and particularly denounced the requirement of church membership as a condition for participating in the communion service, saying, "No church has the the right to establish terms of communion which are not terms of salvation" (Rowdon 1967:9).

One notable attempt to express unity occurred in Birdlington, England, where the Anglican Church decided to erect what they called a Unity Chapel to allow Christians of different persuasions to unite in worship without any imposition of terms on communion that were not specifically stated in Scripture. Local Independents, Baptists, Congregationalists and Anglicans were asked to officiate in the worship. One reason given for this unique experiment illustrates the existing mood that longed for unity:

> The New Testament figures of one fold and one shepherd, a building, a family and a human body show that the followers of Christ should be united in the closest bonds of union. Therefore, the divisions of Christians are the corruptions of Christianity and give rise to intolerance and persecution (Rowdon 1967:11).

This mood toward unity and idealism existed also in the dissenting churches where many were becoming impatient with the sectarianism the dissenting churches promoted. A spontaneous movement began both in the British Isles and in America where those dissatisfied with the current situation of the church tried to reverse the tide of separatism. Many formed small congregations with the simple idea of trying to become New Testament churches, meeting every Sunday to break bread, pray, and praise the Lord, listen to admonishment from the Scriptures and take a collection for the poor. Common threads linked these congregations: they were governed by a plurality of elders; they would not accept the idea of a clergy because it was incompatible with Scripture— which was regarded as their only authority (ibid:23-24).

Unfortunately, idealism soon faded and even these "New Testament churches" began to divide and deteriorate. Although it is difficult to establish a direct connection between these groups that sprang up between 1800-1830 and the later Brethren renewal movement, still the spontaneous nature of their emergence indicates a mood toward idealism and unity that was abroad. This mood, however, lacked leadership and direction— which eventually was provided by those who became known as "The Brethren from Plymouth."

Brethren history points out the importance and role the study of prophecy had in formulating the Brethren from Plymouth. William Neatby, an early chronicler of Brethren history, said, "Brethrenism is the child of the study of unfulfilled prophecy and of the expectation of the immediate return of the Savior" (1901:339). It should be pointed out that the original Brethren from Plymouth were people of their day. In the early decades of the 19th century, prophecy was the hottest and most debated doctrinal issue in the Christian church on both sides of the Atlantic. It was during this period that William Miller, a Baptist preacher and later the originator of the Seventh Day Adventist movement in the United States, was setting specific dates when Jesus Christ would return.

Although the prophetic issue was an important theme which brought the Brethren movement together, later it became the source of division— as well as the forerunner of what became known as Dispensational Theology. This theology formed the substance and structure for the Scofield Reference Bible and constituted one of the most important elements in the history of fundamentalism in the United States (Sandeen 1970:61). From the study of prophecy came a theology of the church which carried the seeds that eventually created the major divisions and many problems that even to this day still characterize those that come from the Brethren tradition.

It is vitally important to realize that throughout the history of the church of Jesus Christ, there has never been a consensus opinion among those who love the Lord and are committed to the Word of God concerning prophetic interpretation. Where there is no consensus among those who call Jesus Lord and the Word truth, it is wise not to be dogmatic. Interestingly, even the early Brethren were not in agreement on prophetic issues (Coad 1966). George Muller, the man of great faith and of orphanage fame, did not believe in the pretribulation rapture, but he was just one of a number of influential Brethren who did not subscribe to the rapture position (Steer 1975:276).

There was no consensus among early Brethren regarding prophetic matters yet certainly there was unanimous agreement concerning the condition of the church. The Broad Church (Anglican) was too broad because it had become tolerant of sin and corruption. The Narrow Church (dissenting church) was too narrow because it would not accept anyone who was not a member of its particular persuasion. This created the mood toward reform and unity.

Essential to any renewal movement is the spirit of that movement. No person demonstrates this spirit for the Brethren more than Anthony Norris Groves (1775-1853) — whose life illustrates the principles that motivated this movement that spontaneously was breaking upon England and Ireland.

An Anglican dentist by profession from Plymouth, England, upon marriage Groves moved to Exeter where he developed his dental practice and became very successful. Early in his career he wanted to become a missionary but his wife was not so inclined. Not the type to force his idea of God's leading on anyone else, he patiently waited for the Lord to change his wife's heart. His vision and missionary desire, however, remained constant.

During this period he began to realize the needs of the poor in Exeter and with his wife's consent, began to give a tenth of their income to help alleviate some of the poverty around them. This act and the corresponding involvement with the poor caused his wife's faith to come alive. Soon they were giving 25 percent of their income to the poor. The more the Groves got involved in meeting real and practical needs of people, the more committed they became to God. Finally, they decided to keep only that portion of their income they needed to support their family of three children. The rest they gave to the poor as a service to God. From this experience

Groves wrote a remarkable booklet called "Christian Devoted-ness" which details his motto: "labor hard, consume little, give much and all to Christ" (Coad 1966:17). This booklet had great impact on many Christians, especially George Muller.

Meanwhile, Groves' desire to be a missionary continued to grow, and now his wife was solidly behind him. One had to be ordained in the Anglican church to become a full-fledged missionary, so Groves made application and was accepted at Trinity College, Dublin. The current educational system allowed Groves to hire a tutor and study at home, periodically traveling to Dublin to take qualifying examinations for his theological degree.

Coupled with Groves' commitment to Christ was a growing sense of wanting to express, in some way, the deep sense of unity he felt with other believers. While at Trinity College, he met some nonconformist Christians who were also seeking ways to express their unity with the Body of Christ. Anthony Groves was attributed with the following suggestion concerning how their unity might be expressed:

> Believers, meeting together as disciples of Christ, were free to break bread together, as their Lord had admonished them; and that, insofar as the practice of the apostles could be a guide, every Lord's day should be set apart for thus remembering the Lord's death and obeying his parting command (ibid:20).

From this time on, the expression, "to meet in the name of the Lord Jesus only," became a motto conveying the heartfelt need to transcend the sectarian attitudes that were dominant both in the established church and the dissenting churches. The Lord's Supper was clearly perceived as a sacrament of unity.

As Groves continued to prepare for his ordination, he began to question the whole process of ordination, realizing he could not be ordained in the Church of England because he could not sign in good conscience the 39 Articles of Faith. The 37th article stated, "It is lawful for Christian men to take up arms at the command of civil magistrate." Groves held strong convictions against war and felt he could never bear arms— he was determined to go to the mission field and planned to go under the auspices of the Anglican church as a lay missionary. Then he learned that as a lay worker in the church he would not be able to celebrate communion with any of those who had become Christians unless an ordained Anglican clergy was present. This also caused him conflict, for he had come to believe that any believers meeting together in the name of Christ were free to celebrate communion.

Anthony Norris Groves thus became a prototype of those who felt frustrated, wanting to be committed totally to Christ without restrictions. He wanted to serve God but could not without being ordained. He wanted to be a lay missionary but could not worship with the converts unless a cleric was present to administer communion.

The motivating factor driving Groves was freedom— he wanted to be free to express his devotion to God. This spiritual freedom became the glue of the Brethren renewal, holding together those who wanted to express the oneness of the Body of Christ without the restrictive labels of clergy and laity.

Anthony Norris Groves was another who never officially left the Anglican church, even though he had strong reservations about Anglican worship and ordination. One of his closest Anglican clergy friends accused him of separating from the church. Groves' classic reply was:

> You say I quitted *your* communion; if you mean by that I do not now break with the Church of England, this is not true; but if you mean that I do not *exclusively* join, it is quite true, feeling this spirit of exclusiveness to be of the very essence of schism, which the apostle so strongly reproves in the Corinthians. I therefore know no distinction but am ready to break the bread and drink the cup of holy joy with all who love the Lord and will not lightly speak evil of His name. I feel every saint to be a holy person, because Christ dwells in [them] and manifests Himself where [they worship]; and though [their] faults be as many as the hairs of [their] head, my duty still is, with my Lord, to join [them] as a member of the mystical body, and to hold communion and fellowship with [them] in any work of the Lord in which [they] may be engaged. Understand, I do not object to ordination by [persons] if it be exercised on principles consistent with Scripture, but if they think they confer anything more than their permission to preach in their little part of the fold of Christ, I should decline it until they show how they came by that authority from the Word of God, and what are the scriptural rules and limitations of this authority (Coad 1966:23-24).

And so this desire to be the people of God without restriction on one's worship and service began to express itself in a number of places. Dublin, Ireland, is credited with being the first place the Brethren renewal movement began to form. There three separate groups of influential people, each group on the same journey, found each other.

Edward Cronin, a converted Catholic medical student looking for a church to join, became disillusioned by the sectarianism of the dissenting churches. He wanted to enjoy communion with those in the church but was refused because he was not a church member. His conscience was offended, and he refused to become a member because "The Church of God was one, and that all that believe were members of that one body" (Rowdon 1967:38). Soon Cronin found others who felt similarly, and in 1826 and 1827 these began to gather in his home.

A second group was forming around Groves and other local Dublin people. The most prominent figure coming from this group was John Nelson Darby who was not very influential in the early days of the renewal, but who later became the most powerful leader in the Brethren movement. No other single person did more to enhance the movement— some 1,500 churches came into existence as a result of his indefatigable efforts (Coad 1966:106).

As the Brethren renewal movement became a worldwide phenomenon, most of its numerical success came from the work of Darby. Also, through his literature and personal magnetism, he did more to shape modern day dispensationalism than any other person in the 19th century (Sardeen 1970:60f). A portion of his theology is a dominant part of American fundamentalism and evangelicalism even to this day.

The third group which began forming at this time was around an Anglican, John Parnell, who later became a Member of Parliament and was raised to the position of nobility as Lord Congleton.

Eventually, these three groups came together, forming one fellowship in 1830. The Lord's Supper was considered a sacrament of unity and large numbers began to attend their services. To gather in the name of Jesus only was a powerful attraction in those days of sectarianism. But this renewal was also beginning in England where the mood for renewal in the established church was gaining momentum. Debate within the church was centering around the controversial Tractarian or Oxford movement. John Henry Newman urged reform through a return to the Roman church. The established Anglicans wanted to maintain the status quo. No middle ground was to be found until slowly a group of committed evangelicals within the church began to organize.

Among these young and bright Oxonian students was a bright star who eventually became the acknowledged leader— Benjamin Newton from Plymouth. Through Newton's leadership, a dedicated group of evangelical intellectuals began to challenge the Anglican superstructure. On February 6, 1831, a popular Anglican curate, with Newton at his side, preached a famous sermon in the university chapel charging the Anglican church with corruption.

The effects were electrifying. Evangelicals came to the curate's defense as the establishment reacted with bitter attacks. Interestingly, Darby was in attendance that Sunday, heard the sermon and subsequently helped in the defense. When the established church finally disciplined the curate, revoking his ordination, Newton responded by also refusing to be ordained, quitting his position at Oxford shortly before he would have been made a professor at the university. On leaving Oxford Newton went home to Plymouth asking Darby to accompany him. A number of other highly gifted Anglican leaders joined them and the Plymouth renewal had begun.

Newton and the others were successful in tapping the spirit that was yearning for spiritual freedom. Christians wanted to be free to be the people of God without restrictions on their worship or service. Percy Hall, a captain in the King's Navy, was also a highly gifted evangelist. Captain Hall would go wherever he could get an audience and Newton would go along to read the Scriptures. Many became believers through their efforts.

One desire clearly demonstrated at Plymouth was that for unity. In one instance, a wealthy Anglican curate who had resigned his ordination rented an unused chapel and invited anyone, no matter what their religious affiliations might be, to a Bible study. In an attempt at unity, this ex-curate introduced the Lord's Supper at these ecumenical meetings. Darby wrote about them:

> More than once, even with ministers of the national church, we have broken bread on Monday evenings after meeting for Christian edification, where each was free to read, to speak, to pray, or to give out a hymn. Some months afterward, we began to do so on Sunday mornings, making use of the same liberty, only adding the Lord's Supper, which we had and still have, the practice of taking every Sunday (Rowdon 1967:76).

This common thread ran through the early days of the Brethren renewal. There was this innate drive to express the oneness of the Body of Christ around the loaf and cup, for the communion service was seen as the sacrament of unity. The Plymouth renewal grew rapidly. A number of highly educated people with impressive academic credentials joined the movement so leadership gifts were present in abundance.

John Darby, a graduate of Trinity College, Dublin, was a gold medalist in the classical languages. Besides B.W. Newton, there was the Oxonian, G.V. Wigram, who became a renowned Greek and Hebrew scholar. Percy Hall, although not a theologian himself, was the son of the Regius Professor of Religion from Oxford. S.L. Harris, in his late 30s, and thus the oldest of the early Brethren, was an Oxford fellow and a former Anglican clergyperson.

Henry Borlase, a Cambridge graduate and a former Anglican curate, was a powerful writer who became the publisher of the first Brethren magazine, *Christian Witness.* Unfortunately, he died an untimely death in 1835, but had he lived, he might have become the most influential leader of the early Brethren. Henry W. Soltau, a Cambridge lawyer with exceptional leadership ability, produced writings on the tabernacle, the priesthood and the offerings which to this day is considered the standard which Brethren writers have followed. S.P. Tregelles became one of the most respected Greek and Old Testament scholars in all of England.

A church with this kind of youthful leadership was bound to be vibrant for besides these notable scholars, there were many others who were well educated, former Anglicans. With the exception of Harris, all of these mentioned were in their 20s or early 30s. Newton, the acknowledged leader at Plymouth, was only 23 in 1830. They were young people with great vision.

Although to this point in the development of the Brethren renewal all the principal leaders, with the exception of Edward Cronin, had come out of the established church of England or Ireland, it was not long before two prominent leaders came from the dissenting church tradition.

Henry Craik (1805-1866) was born into the Church of Scotland— his father and brothers were all successful academicians and church-persons. The younger Craik found himself discouraged with the established church and after studying for the ministry decided not to accept ordination. As a student at Edinburgh he won numerous academic awards, earning the highest honors in Greek twice during his university career. After turning down the formal clergy profession, Craik turned to independent tutoring, often coaching those who were studying for ordination. In 1826, he accepted a position with a wealthy family in the south of England to tutor the children as well as prepare the father for his ordination exams. The father's name was Anthony Norris Groves.

In England, Craik found time to continue his Greek studies, master Hebrew, and even published a Hebrew grammar. When Groves dropped his plans to finish his ordination exams, Craik accepted other tutorial positions but more and more was drawn into preaching. Soon he accepted the pastorate of a Baptist church in Shaldon where he met the person who would become his best friend, and later his colleague for the Kingdom of God—George Muller.

George Muller (1805-1898), just a month younger than Craik, was to outlive his friend by 32 years. Born in Germany, Muller was raised and confirmed a Lutheran. His early desire was to be a missionary, but constant conflict with his father over financial support caused Muller to leave Germany and go to London for training as a missionary to the Jews. While intensely studying Hebrew, be became ill and was advised by his teachers to convalesce in the country. He went to Teignmouth, just across the river from Shaldon where he met Henry Craik.

From that point on his life was never the same. Through Craik, Muller came to know Anthony Norris Groves. Groves, because of his experience in the Anglican church, began to have a powerful effect on Muller who like Groves, was questioning the lack of freedom in the established church to serve and worship God. Muller finally broke with the missionary society when he perceived them as being too directive—they had restricted him to preach only to the Jews.

With the example of Groves who had gone out as a missionary without ordination from the church and without a fixed financial support before him, Muller decided to separate from the missionary society and follow the lead of his newfound friend, Craik, becoming the pastor of a Baptist church in Teignmouth.

With so much in common it was inevitable that Craik and Muller become lifelong friends. They were the same age, had university educations and loved Hebrew. Both were preachers, although it was commonly acknowledged that Craik was by far the better scholar and preacher. Together the two began to dream about what an ideal local church would be like, longing to be free to follow the Scriptures without any denominational restrictions, expressing the unity of the Body of Christ without sectarian biases. Before the Brethren in Plymouth had organized, both Muller and Craik were moving toward a position of freedom of worship and service (Rowdon 1967:14).

The opportunity came to them when Craik was invited to be a pastor of an independent chapel in Bristol which meant having access to an unused chapel called Bethesda, which was seen as an overflow building for projected future growth. Craik accepted the invitation on the conditions that he could bring his friend, George Muller, along to help with the work and that they would not be considered the pastors of the church but ministering brethren. A final stipulation was that they would not be given a fixed salary nor would pew rents be countenanced.*

Soon the people in Bristol realized Henry Craik was one of the finest preachers around and tremendous crowds came to hear him preach. Bethesda Chapel no longer was an unused building and the renewal movement was in full swing in Bristol. Eventually, numerous core churches came into existence.

Interestingly history records that as early as October, 1832, John Darby preached at Bethesda Chapel thus establishing an early connection between the Dublin, Plymouth and Bristol Brethren (loc cit).

Of course we must admit that it was not the popularity of Craik's preaching or later Muller's loving concern seen in the establishment of the Ashley Downs orphanages that accounted for the phenomenal growth of the Bristol Brethren renewal. Here, too, the Spirit of God was working in the hearts of the people of God. The desire for freedom to worship and serve God in the name of Jesus only was sweeping England and Ireland wherever the Spirit listeth.

---

* It was common practice for established and dissenting churches to raise money by levying fees for one's place at the pew.

Consolidating the Renewal

5

The network of connections between the Irish Brethren and the English Brethren kept growing. Groves was a primary figure here because he was connected to the Dublin Brethren through Trinity College and yet was tied in with the Oxford movement because Francis Newman, John Henry Newman's brother, went with him to the mission field. Groves was connected to the Bristol Brethren, through Henry Craik, his tutor, and George Muller married Groves' sister. His own father lived with the Muller family for many years. While relationally Anthony Groves became a living prototype for renewal, theologically the study of prophecy became the academic magnet that drew the young movement together.

In the late 1820s there had been a series of conferences held in Albury, England for the purpose of studying the prophetic teaching of the Bible. Special attention was given to the study of Revelation and to the nation of Israel. During one of these conferences a new idea emerged concerning the Lord Jesus' return: someone suggested that there was an inherent difference between the appearing of Christ and the second coming of Christ.* One, the appearance of Christ in the sky was for the purpose of resurrecting the dead in Christ and the translation of the living saints (1 Th 4:16-17); whereas the advent of Christ was seen as the event when Christ

---

* This is the first reference to the rapture of the church mentioned in history with the possible exception of a third- or fourth-century theologian named Victorinus (Coad 1966:22).

comes back to earth a King, bringing judgment to the nations and establishing his kingdom on earth.

A number of influential people attended these conferences, including Lady Theodosia Powerscourt, the widow of Lord Powerscourt from Ireland, who was intensely interested in prophecy. When the Albury conferences ended, she sponsored a subsequent conference on prophecy back at her estate in Powerscourt, Ireland. It was to these conferences that John Nelson Darby and the Dublin Brethren came, as well as some of the Plymouth and Bristol Brethren.

At first these conferences had the sanction of the established church since Lady Powerscourt was a dedicated Anglican. As time went by and the experiences of Oxford, Dublin and Plymouth became more of a factor in the lives of these Brethren, they began to threaten the established church. At the second Powerscourt conference the subject of apostasy and the established church was even addressed publicly. At this time Darby and others began to argue for a withdrawal from the state church, and shortly after the second conference, Lady Powerscourt joined the Dublin Brethren, withdrawing from the Anglican church.

By the third Powerscourt conference the established church was conspicuously absent and the Brethren were definitely in control. Some 400 people attended, drawn both by a widespread disillusionment with the established and dissenting churches and by a great interest in the study of prophecy. To John Darby these two issues fit perfectly together. The established church, as well as all other forms of independent church life constituted Christendom— which was the Babylon of the book of Revelation— the symbol of the Antichrist system which was opposed to the life and work of the true church. The only valid response was to withdraw from the apostasy.

At this time Darby was in heated debate with the Church of Ireland and wrote a polemical pamphlet entitled "The Notion of a Clergyman: Dispensationally the Sin Against the Holy Ghost" (Coad 1966:83). Although there was general agreement among the Brethren concerning the situation of the church, many— including Henry Craik, George Muller, and Anthony Norris Groves— would not take such a polemical stand as Darby toward other churches.

The principal Brethren all met at the third Powerscourt conference. Representing the Plymouth Brethren were B.W. Newton and Captain Percy Hall; George Muller and Henry Craik were there from Bristol; and many Dublin Brethren were there, including

John Darby who had become their spokesperson. Important to note is the fact that, while there was a consensus of opinion concerning the condition of the church, there was no consensus concerning the interpretation of the prophecy.

All the Brethren were futurists, believing the book of Revelation was yet to be fulfilled, but not all had accepted the idea of a two-stage advent, and the question of separating the advent of Christ into a rapture and second coming was still hotly debated. At this point even John Darby had not made up his mind. Historically, this is a curious phenomena, for in many circles John Darby has been credited or accused— depending upon one's own eschatological beliefs— of being the originator of the doctrine of the rapture of the church, but clearly he was not.

In fact, in the early days of the Brethren renewal, there was a great deal of tolerance shown on this point of doctrine. The Dublin Brethren, by and large, held the two-stage advent position, whereas the Plymouth Brethren were divided. It is recorded even that Percy Hall would preach on the theme of the rapture on Sunday morning and in the evening Wigram would preach against it (Rowdon 1967:82). Eventually this conflict stopped when Hall, an evangelist at heart, moved to Hereford to help plant a church in that area.

Although there was a difference in the interpretation of prophecy, the Brethren allowed for that and, at least in the early days, maintained a warm fellowship with those whose futuristic interpretations differed from their own. The Brethren in Plymouth supported Hall in his church planting ministry, while the leadership at Bristol, by and large, did not accept the secret rapture position. However, both positions were held and caused no disruption of fellowship. Apparently, prophetic truth was not regarded as nonnegotiable.

The Powerscourt conference of 1833 became a landmark because there for the first time the three principal centers of Brethren renewal were brought together. In order to seal the sense of unity, Lady Powerscourt invited the inner circle— Darby and Bellett from Dublin; Craik and Muller from Bristol; Hall and Newton from Plymouth— to her garden house to celebrate the Lord's Supper— still regarded as the symbol of unity.

And so, by the late 1830s, the Brethren renewal movement spread phenomenally. Congregations were formed in London, Dublin and throughout the area around Bristol and Plymouth.

Groves had gone to India, Darby to Europe. The freedom and unity movement was catching on everywhere and was seen as a remarkable moving of the Spirit of God.

The Brethren Movement Today

6

The next hundred years saw the Brethren movement grow and flourish, spreading the good news of Christ around the world. Churches were established and missionaries were sent forth to the uttermost regions. The pioneers of the church had a vision that carried it forth. Their enthusiasm was infectious.

Regardless of such historical success, *all is not well today* in the Brethren renewal movement. The apogee has passed. In fact, recent surveys have shown a startling decline. In 1981, International Crusades (now called International Teams) conducted a telephone survey of over 1,100 assemblies (local churches) to ascertain the health and strength of the Brethren in North America. This is of vital concern to International Teams since the Brethren form their primary pool from which short-term missionaries are recruited.

By asking the various assemblies questions about their size, vitality and program, the following statistics were tabulated: 23 percent of the assemblies were progressing and growing; 25 percent were holding their own; 26 percent were either defunct, dead or dying. The final 26 percent were classified as tight assemblies— a descriptive label of a subgroup (found in the open assembly address book) which means they form their own close-knit or tight fellowship and have little, if any, cooperation with the larger body of open Brethren. Generally, these tight assemblies are very conservative and quite small in size. All observable evidence indicates that they are declining rapidly. So, practically, this indicates that over half of the Brethren assemblies listed in the address book are either dead or in a declining situation.

Another recent written survey done by a graduate student at Wheaton College confirms the International Teams survey. Under the title, "A Pilot Study of Open Plymouth Brethren Assemblies in North America Responsive to Change," the author surveyed assemblies responsive to change—immediately eliminating almost a third of the assemblies listed in the "1983 Address Book of Some Assemblies of Christians" because these were deemed unresponsive to change by the International Teams.

International Teams experience also showed that those assemblies which designate their buildings "Gospel Halls" tend to be the so-called "tight assemblies" and it is safe to assume they are more conservative and less responsive to change and to research questionnaires (Fleming, 1984:3). The remaining assemblies were sent an extensive six-page questionnaire to which 51 percent responded. By adding the nonresponsive group to the eliminated group, some 64 percent of those listed in the assembly address book were not included in this study. This does not necessarily mean that almost two-thirds of the assemblies in North America are not uninterested in change, but it does confirm the International Teams' conclusions drawn from their telephone survey which showed that over half of the assemblies currently listed can be regarded as listless.

Those that responded to Fleming's questionnaire constitute 36 percent of the listed assemblies. In an encouraging vein, some 94 percent of those responding assemblies felt they were prepared to make changes while another 96 percent indicated a desire to grow (ibid:14). But the desire for change and growth, unfortunately, does not produce change and growth. Those surveyed, which must be considered the most open to change and progressive in structure, have a growth of 2.4 percent per year. This growth factor, when coupled with the apparent decline in the other 64 percent of the assemblies, becomes extremely discouraging (ibid:xi).

Further analysis of the statistics about this 36 percent group leads to even more pessimism: Less than a quarter of those considered to be the most open to change and growth added more than 15 people to their assembly in the past five years! This includes additions of any kind—new converts, transfers from other assemblies, transfers from other denominations or even the children of present members (ibid:33). Two-thirds of these progressive assemblies have no college or career groups and 77 percent of them have no fellowship aimed at young married couples (ibid:23). Only 29 percent of this group have elders or full-time workers engaged in pastoral visitations (ibid:43) and 46 percent of them have less than 35 people at the Lord's Supper each Sunday (ibid:24). So while an encouraging 94 percent desire change, of these only 14 percent thought that change should involve leadership training and/or handing over the leadership to the young (ibid:52). This, in spite of the fact that the single greatest issue facing the assemblies, according to this research thesis, is leadership (ibid:51).

These two surveys would indicate that the Plymouth Brethren, as an identifiable Christian tradition in North America, is in trouble. Unfortunately, these statistics cannot be viewed dispassionately by those of us who owe a great deal to the rich Brethren tradition with its vision of the Body of Christ that is unique to Christendom. Even though these statistics are bleak and painful to face, criticism and the most intense scrutiny, no matter how severe, must not be feared. Truth will stand. Our belief in the unity of the Body of Christ, the centrality of worship and the priesthood of all believers— the principles that motivated the original Brethren renewal in England in the 1830s— are as valid and applicable today as they were then, and as they were in the first century.

But in order to make these truths valid and applicable today, we must be open and honest before God and before each other. Our motivation must come from a pure heart, a good conscience and a faith without hypocrisy (I Tm 1:5).

With such positive motivation, coupled with a longing for renewal among God's people found especially in congregations that come from the Plymouth Brethren tradition, we can ask God to help us as we work for renewal. It is my deep conviction that there are many people in congregations across the land praying for renewal. Even though this volume is dedicated to those seeking renewal within the Plymouth Brethren tradition, still the principles are valid for all who seek God's face, fresh every morning.

We cannot ignore the disturbing nature of these two surveys. There is always something cold and impersonal about statistics and percentages. Percentages and numbers are not leaving the Brethren assemblies; people are. Statistics are not staying in the assemblies; people are. Quantitative surveys like these are needed and the information they produced I found extremely valuable, but this information was limited. In fact, I found these surveys only whetted my appetite. I wanted to know the answers to the next logical obvious questions: Why is there a decline in the assemblies? Why are people leaving? What are the sources of disaffection that cause people to leave?

These questions need to be addressed if we are to discover the reasons behind the exodus that is taking place in the assemblies across North America. Consequently, I concluded that what is needed is a qualitative survey that probes the motives behind those statistics and so I began my own study to explore the sources of disaffection within the Plymouth Brethren assemblies.

It seemed a logical place to start with interviews of those who had left the assemblies. It also seemed wise to interview selected elders and leaders who are still currently involved in ministry within the assemblies. It is one thing to ask those who have left, it is quite a different matter to interview elders and leaders and ask them why they believe people are leaving the Brethren.

These personal interviews followed the analytical inductive method as propounded by Denzin (1970) and Schwartz (1979). The interviews were inductive because they involved face-to-face discussions without any preconceived suppositions as to why anyone leaves the Brethren. The survey was also analytical because each interview was taped and then analyzed so as to discover the sources of disaffection, and then these sources of disaffection were compared and contrasted with preceding interviews in order to categorize and record them.

In all, 52 people were interviewed—39 who had already left the Brethren and 13 current leaders in the Brethren movement, including five full-time commended workers in North America. Almost all the 39 who had left had been leaders in their assemblies, and most are today leaders in their present churches. Of the 52, some 22 were from California, 13 from the Northwest (Portland, Seattle, and Vancouver, BC); 12 were from the Midwest and five were from the Northeast. Although not all the regions of North America are represented, still a fair sampling of the four primary pockets of Brethren assemblies were surveyed.

Almost everyone interviewed has had a long personal history with the Brethren. In fact, 36 were second- to fourth-generation Brethren. Of the 16 first-generation people, only two had been with the Brethren for less than seven years. The rest had been with the assemblies most of their adult life. This underscores the point that these people are not young idealists who have been to Bible school and are seeking the perfect church. They are committed Christians with a long history with the Brethren. The youngest people interviewed were those in their 30s, but these already had established families; the oldest were grandparents approaching 70. Of the group, 35 were college graduates, eight held master's degrees and five had earned doctorates.

Those interviewed were clearly not a cross section of the Brethren— they were and are leaders in the Body of Christ— people with a lot to say. My interest was not just academic. I went to listen, ask questions and record what they said because I personally wanted to discover the answers. My purpose now is essentially to rebroadcast their story without acting as their interpreter. I assured them all anonymity but they knew what they said might be used in this paper.

This is thus their story— at times critical, sometimes even bitter. But this criticism and even the cynicism still conveys to us a message that needs to be heard. One other important point to emphasize is that while the vast majority of the recorded comments are negative and critical in nature, most of them come within the context of a lot of feeling and love. In a strange way, those who have left the Brethren, for the most part, still feel a deep love and respect for their heritage. In fact, a former elder from an assembly in the Midwest best summarized the attitude of those interviewed:

> Our love for the people in the assemblies is as great as it has ever been. We do not feel any animosity. We feel a sense of failure. Maybe we did not do all we could to work toward renewal. It would be exciting if there was a bona fide renewal among the Brethren.

The Interviewee's Viewpoints

7

What follows, then, is the story told me by these people. My task was to act as a chronicler and categorizer, at times an editor— but never with intent of altering the sense of what was told me.

Interestingly enough, as these stories were being categorized, three sources of disaffection were by far the most common reasons given as to why people are leaving the Plymouth Brethren assemblies:

Lack of Positive Leadership

Here the interviews affirmed the findings of the cited written survey done by Lois Fleming. ("The single greatest issue facing the assemblies is leadership" ibid:51). The interviews not only confirmed this analysis but also pointed out that the single greatest reason people give for leaving the assemblies is the lack of positive leadership, and then the other sources of disaffection flow from this main problem.

Three influential elders from the Chicago area confirmed this and one even said, "The greatest problem facing the assemblies today is knowing what to do with nonfunctional elders." A former commended worker from California said in regards to the elders he had worked with:

> They will neither lead nor follow nor get out of the way. They feel they have a sacred trust given to them to perpetuate what they think used to be the good old days.

Another elder who left and is currently a leader in a parachurch organization said, "There is no procedure for selecting, evaluating and dismissing elders." An elder from Oregon who had left his assembly flatly confirmed, "Weak and insensitive leadership is the main reason people leave the assembly."

Unfortunately, most of the time these nonfunctional elders represent a rigidity and inflexibility that is stifling and counter-productive to good leadership in the assembly. The question as to how these nonfunctional elders came to power was unclear to many. One older Brethren, converted through an assembly evangelist, said, "After 39 years in the assembly, I have no idea how elders are chosen." Another said, "Elders are chosen by seniority, faithful attendance and consistent ideology with the other elders." A successful professional who was also a third-generation Brethren observed:

> After the real elders died, in the period of five years others became elders strictly on the basis of their age, time and rank. Frankly, they did not have it and they would not step aside. They preached an archaic, old-fashioned line and the younger, more talented men left.

The wife of a former elder made an insightful observation that also may be true of many Brethren assemblies. She said:

> Our assembly came out of a tight assembly background and we retained some of the exclusive tendencies, such as the nonrecognition of elders. This created real problems because when we began to recognize elders, there were men who had been there for 50 years. They just assumed leadership roles and there was no way to get these men out.

Not only is it extremely difficult to remove nonfunctional elders, often these same elders are the most rigid. A former elder from the Northwest said, "The inability to question teaching or policy or even ask questions innocently without being classed a heretic or a rebel was so real that no one dared."

A mother in her 30s, whose husband came from a long line of Brethren and is now active as an elder in an independent church, essentially agreed concerning the rigidity of the elders. The issue that finally caused them to leave was over women and head coverings. She stated:

> After all the seemingly objective discussion of the passages and the doctrine, it really boiled down to a question of submission to the elders. Then we began to think of all the really important doctrinal

issues in the Bible to discuss, yet the one in which our spirituality was being judged was the head covering doctrine. It dawned on us: If this is the way they are going to view *this* issue, then we are not sure we want to entrust our entire spiritual life and future to someone who sees issues in this way.

Incidentally, when this extremely active couple left the assembly, almost an entire generation of young adults and young married people followed them. Today their former assembly is a shell of what it used to be.

Because leadership is often so rigid and inflexible, little change is ever seen. This also stifles vision. Over and over, this fact was repeated in the interviews. A commended worker in an assembly in the Northeast said:

> We need a change in leadership. The leadership must reflect a younger generation. Too often the leadership in the assemblies is too old and too insecure. As others have pointed out, the leadership is motivated by fear. They are afraid of change, afraid to do anything. We need a younger, more vigorous leadership in the church.

A former deacon and activist in a Los Angeles assembly who today is an elder in a large independent church said of his former assembly:

> The leadership was self-appointed; they were not congregationally appointed. The elders propagated themselves without any congregational input. They simply were not sensitive to the needs of the people and there was no effort to bring younger men into the group.

A bright and successful businessperson who would have been a future leader in his assembly was asked to speak at an elders-deacons' retreat. He commented on this:

> I led a seminar at an elders-deacons' retreat on goal setting. I was excited because the Scriptures are filled with admonitions on this subject. There was a group of 35, maybe 50, men at this discussion. I made a 45-minute presentation. When I was through, I got some of the dumbest questions I ever heard in my life. The questions reflected an attitude like, why should we plan? What's the necessity of setting goals? And at the same time they were asking questions like, why is the attendance down? Why aren't we seeing growth in the assembly? I thought to myself, these are our leaders! They don't have any vision at all.

One factor which inhibits change and increased vision in the assemblies is the prevalence of the unanimity principle in decision-making. In practice, this becomes the rule of the minority, since it is almost impossible to move forward with any unanimity. If one or two elders hold the whole assembly back, this produces resentment and a constant feeling of division and strife. An elder in a Midwest assembly affirmed this when he said:

> A couple of the elders are not open to change and new ideas. Consequently, we have a five-to-two split. Generally, we follow the rule of yielding to one another, but when it comes to important issues, it boils down to a rule by the minority.

This rule by the verbal minority was classically illustrated in another story:

> A number in the assembly, plus a lot of the college-age young people, wanted the midweek prayer meeting to be held in homes as well as in the chapel. This point was being lobbied for during a men's meeting when one of the venerable old stalwarts, a foundational member and elder of the congregation, got up and said, "If we divide up the assembly into home prayer groups, we will be cutting the heart right out of the assembly." After that, the proposal never had a chance, even though the majority were for it.

A former commended worker held another opinion that the leadership is still in such disarray among the Brethren because the teaching of John Nelson Darby still has a powerful effect in the assemblies. He felt that Darby's doctrine of the church in ruin, which soundly condemns any and all organization, still causes elders to be suspicious of organization within the church. Another who had left one of the largest and most progressive assemblies in Southern California seemed to agree:

> Good leadership utilizes the resources of the church to the fullest. That was not happening at our chapel. When you are a do-it-yourself church, you must be organized. In comparison to the church we are going to now, our assembly was not organized at all . . .

> Organization at our chapel was looked upon in a negative way because if you were organized, you were really not letting God's Spirit lead . . . The biggest surprise that I have seen in the eight months being in this new church is the number of people using their gifts. It is really exciting. The percentage is so much higher than in our assembly. At the Chapel, ten percent of the people do 90 percent

of the work. I was told when we were considering leaving that all the churches are that way. That simply has not been true in our experience.*

In spite of these prevalent views, one of the primary problems that faces the future of the Brethren movement is how to provide that needed leadership. Some assemblies have faced the problem of leadership, making significant progress at correcting the situation. One general observation heard a number of times which seemed to ring true was that where there is flexible leadership on the part of the elders and/or a full-time worker, that assembly tends to show vitality and growth. An elder in a large and progressive assembly in a suburb of Chicago confirmed this:

> Our assembly is growing because we have been characterized as an assembly that is open to change. This is manifest to the community by the type of services we have. One word that characterizes us would be "Flexibility."

When pushed for details, he went on to say:

> We have a full-time elder who acts as an administrator. A significant part of our growth is attributed to this. Also, our elders are open to change. As a group, we are committed and there is a unity of purpose in the group. We also keep open communication with the congregation through open forums and written evaluation surveys.

Lack of Vitality

Because the Plymouth Brethren in North America are declining, one would not only expect to see a definite lack of vitality, but also link this lack to their leadership problem. This lack of vibrancy is seen in every aspect of the corporate life of the assembly according to the interviews, but especially produces a general attitude of discouragement, a specific dissatisfaction with the quality of ministry and worship and, finally, a growing sense of disillusionment with regard to the place of women in the assembly.

Once I asked a former commended worker why he had left the assemblies. His startling response was, "I have not left the Brethren movement; the Brethren assemblies have left the Brethren move-

---

* Further verbatim comments illustrating the current leadership crisis are cited in Appendix A under "Lack of Positive Leadership."

ment. They no longer practice the Brethren principles." He spoke not only from his understanding of Brethren principles but also from his experience of having circulated regularly in about 35 assemblies in California.

A totally different perspective was expressed by a third-generation ex-Brethren who had come from a very prominent family in Brethren circles. He said of his local situation, "There is no real dissatisfaction with the Brethren per se but a definite dissatisfaction with this particular assembly."

Similar statements were iterated often. In fact, one academician made this statement, "If there was an alive assembly like... or like... in the area, we would still be in the Brethren." The address book lists eight assemblies within a reasonable driving distance from this person's home. A grandmother who has been active in children's work in her home for over 28 years said, "It was hard to leave but harder to stay. When I began to develop a critical spirit, I knew it was time to leave."

Personal perspectives definitely color the situation. One former leader and elder, who travels all over the world in his work, made this comment:

> All you need to do is open your eyes. I've traveled around the world many times. I've gone to many parts of the world and if you have any idea of what is happening around the world today, you will see that renewal is happening in the so-called charismatic movement. It has overtaken the world—in South America, Africa and parts of the Orient. There is an openness and there is a joy, but people here in the assemblies have their heads in the sand.

From such a world viewpoint to the local situation, there is an attitude of discouragement. One gifted woman, both an author and speaker in the broader Body of Christ, said about her past assembly situation, "We felt hopeless. We'd go Sunday after Sunday and I would cry all the way home. We were struggling with the deadness."

Another reflected an attitude heard often and said, "It is a real drag to make yourself go. We began to look for excuses to miss the midweek meeting." A former elder on the West coast said, "We felt the Holy Spirit was being squelched. There just didn't seem to be any life." Even more specific was former elder in the Chicago area who said:

> The emphasis in the assembly was on form, not content. You had to do it this way whether there was any life in it or not, and in most

instances there was not any life in it. When it came to feeling and experiencing the joy of the Lord and the presence of the Lord and the power of the Lord, it is just not there in the assembly. We were experiencing this but not in the assembly.

Such discouragement has led many to feel personally burned-out especially if they have put a lot of effort into reversing the declining situation.*

A declining assembly whose level of vitality is down, tends to ignore relational problems and gloss over hypocrisy. This was powerfully substantiated by a returned missionary in a Chicago-area assembly:

As Christians we live often in a phony world and we are afraid to admit failure. Failure should not be a part of the Christian life. The truth of the matter is when one member suffers, the other members suffer. But we aren't genuine. We go there Sunday after Sunday with our heads covered and our pious faces. We moan and groan about our sins in a very abstract way, never confessing our real sins but just sins in general. We talk about our sins that nailed the Lord Jesus to the cross and yet in the same meeting parents are refusing to speak to their (grown) children, children refuse to speak to the parents, spouses are living in an angry state with each other. These same people moan and groan about our sin at the Lord's Supper and all the time deny that we have any sin— it is all very sad.

Almost every person surveyed is either a leader in their present church or they were elders or leaders in their former assemblies. Although the quality of pulpit ministry was rarely the main source of dissatisfaction, a number expressed strong feelings on the subject. A former elder summarized the thinking of many who had left when he said: "The preaching is hit or miss. It is very erratic. At its highest point, it was very good. At its lowest point it was painful. The ministry is characterized by great unevenness. The amazing thing to me was the ministry committee seemed ignorant of the problem."

Ignoring the issue seems to be common. An elder from the Northwest said, "The strongest aspect of our assembly is the heavy emphasis on the teaching ministry . . . The pulpit ministry is very

---

* More comments illustrating the general discouragement and burnout are under "Lack of Vitality" in Appendix A.

good." Yet another potential leader of that very assembly who had left took a totally different perspective and said, "We were never challenged from the pulpit to be thinking Christians. The whole congregation suffered from that."

An active former member concurred:

> There wasn't any capable in-house ministry. Ninety percent of the ministry was imported. There were in-house people who could stand up in the pulpit but they were untrained. They loved the Lord, but this problem became greater as the congregation became more educated.

This situation creates problems. One elder who went to another church for a year because of a temporary business move, commented:

> The Lord showed us how mediocre the ministry is in our assembly. We began to see how routine and elementary the preaching is… On several occasions I suggested to the other elders that we go and visit some alive churches. They would not do that.

So compounding the exposure to quality ministry taking place in the broader Body of Christ is the fact that more and more people in the assemblies are becoming better educated and thus less tolerant of untrained preachers. A former Brethren, whose father is still a Brethren preacher and whose grandfather was a full-time worker observed:

> If you are a thinking person, you are more demanding of the teaching that one gets from the pulpit. You are unwilling to listen to rigid adherence to the party line. You want to hear something that is stimulating, something that will cause you to think and make choices.*

Listless Worship Services

The centrality of worship as a doctrine and open participatory communion as a practice are major distinctives of the Plymouth

---

* A number of highly educated elders and full-time workers as well as those who have left the Brethren have made some technical, yet practical observations as to the quality and vitality of the pulpit ministry which are listed in Appendix A under "Dissatisfaction with the Pulpit Ministry."

Brethren. It is hard to overemphasize the place of worship in the assemblies. A former full-time worker related:

> I once asked a distinguished Christian leader how to change a church and he said, "Identify the sacred cow and then never attack it." So I have never attacked the narrowness of the Brethren concept of worship.

While this is true for those who are on the inside, it is not true for those who have left the Brethren and who maintain strong opinions and feelings about the open communion tradition in which they were raised.

A host of these feelings commented on the deadness of the communion service. A former elder's wife said,

> The joyous worship of the Lord was missing in the Breaking of Bread. When you look in the Old Testament and you see the use of instruments and the joyous worship of God in a full way, you realize something is missing in our worship. We only remembered Jesus or more properly *the* Lord Jesus Christ and there was not much joy. We were longing for some emotion. We were sick spiritually, emotionally and physically. We were dying and we had to leave.

This same idea was expressed by a former assembly activist from the Chicago area who said,

> Brethren worship is too intellectual, too cerebral. There is no appeal to the intuitive or the imaginative side of our being. This is left to starve. The fact of the matter is you cannot worship apart from the Spirit.

A large number of comments directed at the worship service focused upon the predictability and the inflexibility of the meeting. The following are characteristic:

> Sometimes there was spontaneity in the worship meeting, but the majority of the time you knew who was going to give out the next hymn or prayer. It was always the same. It was a format.

> The Lord's Supper was tedious, monotonous and boring. It was unstructured but really structured.

> I originally enjoyed the worship. But after you've been there awhile, the same men would do everything and it got to be rote. It was done the same way, never anything new or spontaneous or joyous.

> The absolute narrowness, in my opinion, of the definition of worship was exceedingly stifling. The attitude that worship must be pure,

therefore there should be no musical instruments, was nonsense to me.

At the Breaking of Bread I have heard many tape-recorded prayers. To me it was like we were so dead and so much in a rut. We were all for forms and appearances and for going through this particular routine.*

An unwritten assumption about the worship meeting is that it acts as a spirituality barometer. This creates tremendous pressures and expectations on participants and also bears some bitter fruit among those who have left.

One extremely active couple who were involved in youth work taught Sunday school and were involved in the midweek programs. They had both graduated from a three-year Bible school program. On occasion the husband would take his turn on the platform where his gifts were generally very well received. Yet he said:

No matter how much you did, your spirituality was measured by your attendance at the Lord's Supper... Attendance at that meeting is used as an indicator of one's spiritual condition. If a person wants to speak in public and he doesn't participate at the Lord's Supper, two things happen: First, there is suspicion you may not have what it takes (public gift); second, there is no exposure and without that exposure, there is no other path to the platform. . . .

Other people did get opportunities (to preach at the Family Bible Hour) who were less gifted than I, in my opinion, simply because I did not participate at the Lord's Supper. The rule is the more spontaneous at the Lord's Supper, the more opportunities for speaking. I really felt there was a political kind of power thing you had to go through if you wanted to get ahead.

Another former Brethren astutely commented on the pressure often experienced by communion service participants.

I felt for a long time that an awful lot of the very visible people in the Brethren are people who seemed to be unfulfilled by reason of their secular activities. So when they come to the church activities, especially the Lord's Supper, they can talk and they can talk incessantly.

---

* Other strong feelings about the worship service are recorded in Appendix A under "Lack of Vitality."

If one's visibility and verbalizing at worship become a spiritual status symbol, then those seeking that will be participating all the more. Conversely, if you are not a participant, then something must be spiritually amiss. One person said,

> I was told more than once that something was wrong with me because I didn't want to stand up at the Breaking of Bread. I was told if you don't enjoy that meeting, something was wrong with you. To participate meant you were spiritual, especially if you got emotional. I could not do it. I would sit there and I tried to work on my feelings. I just couldn't.

The question of the vitality in worship was also asked of the active elders and commended workers. All but one acknowledged serious problems concerning the communion service. Even the one who saw nothing that needed changing at the Breaking of Bread acknowledged puzzlement over the drop in attendance. They commonly experienced 300-350 at the Family Bible Hour yet under 150 at the worship service. His explanation for the drop in attendance was:

> Those who don't attend do not think it is important. Their priorities are set in such a way so as to exclude worship. I just do not understand why what I value so much is not valued by all.

Yet it was from this very assembly some of the sharpest criticism came concerning the worship service. In fact, the harshest critique came from those of his own family who had left.

An elder from the Bay area of Northern California commented on this topic:

> My personal feeling is that what began as a very wonderful expression of worship has been reduced to a set of regulations where all we have is form. We are holding to form as though it were biblical. It is a real blind spot. Jesus said, "Remember me." He did not leave us a form. We have to find alternative ways to obey the Lord and remember Him by breaking free from this mold. We need to be creative and encourage spontaneity.

Another elder from a suburban assembly said:

> The weakest aspect of our service is worship. I feel badly about that. In the early days I remember its being our strength. At our chapel, people don't seem to come prepared to the worship service. They are not ready to participate. At the most, it is the same ten men. The women can't participate and the men don't for whatever reason.

When asked further how he saw the worship meeting, he said, "Unfortunately, I find that meeting to be very dry, a very dead meeting and I don't know what to do about it."

Surprisingly, another elder from this assembly, who is a commended worker with considerable influence among the broader Brethren constituency, expressed an altogether different perspective. His unique view is that the Brethren distinctive is not the centrality of worship as seen in a participatory communion but rather it is the remembrance as seen in an open participatory communion. Remembrance is worship but worship can be much broader than remembrance. He stated:

> The problem develops when people begin to identify the communion service as the worship service as if that were the only form of worship. Then you have a stress because people who have been raised in a traditional Brethren setting are used to a remembrance meeting where the form of thought is on the sufferings of the Lord Jesus Christ or the character of the Savior or something to do with redemption. Then people get very frustrated when someone breaks the mood. Someone comes along and wants to share his experience or young people hear a lot about sharing and body life and they want to express that. Since the Breaking of Bread is the only participatory meeting, they assume it is the place to express these things.

He went on to say that these two aspects of worship could not be brought together: "Our distinctive is remembrance and not worship in the broad sense."

Another elder, a commended worker on the West coast, made a pertinent contrasting comment:

> This attitude, to a greater or lesser degree, has always been in the assemblies. The attitude in effect says that we are the ones who worship right. We do it biblically and we are the ones who practice the priesthood of all believers and we are the ones who practice the leading of the Holy Spirit and we are the ones who have the form that is truly biblical.

A resident commended worker from the East coast observed concerning the Lord's Supper:

> What we have done is taken an informal format designed for a home setting in the first century and we have put it into a formal setting in a sanctuary in a church building in the 20th century. The two clash. We either need to change the structure of the Lord's Supper to make it formal to fit the contemporary setting or change the setting to

make it informal so as to go along with the biblical format of the Lord's supper . . .

My own feeling about the way most assemblies remember the Lord, with an open format in a building sitting in rows as we do, is that we emphasize our individualism. We worship as individuals without any horizontal connections. We simply speak vertically and individually. It becomes more of a performance. In my opinion, many of these meetings self-destruct because it gives people an opportunity to work out their own neuroses.*

Closely related to the dissatisfaction with the quality of worship is the whole question concerning women and their place in the Brethren assemblies.

Marginalized Women in the Assembly

A number of both men and women were critical of the position that the assemblies take regarding women. Typical comments follow here.

One woman, married into an assembly family, observed:

My impression as a woman coming into the assemblies was you did not participate at all. Being a woman meant you were to serve. You were expected to be on the kitchen committee, go to wedding and baby showers, as well as all the meetings. You had to make sure you had your hat on and that was it. There was no opportunity for me to share with anybody publicly. I just had to keep everything inside . . .

I tried to ask questions but soon learned certain questions should not be asked, questions like, Why could only men take part in the Breaking of Bread? Why were the women to be silent? When I asked that question, I was told that the New Testament silences women. When I asked about all the other New Testament references about women praying, teaching and prophesying, I was told we aren't even to ask those sorts of questions.

These particular issues and related problems were prime factors causing some younger married couples to leave the assemblies. One talented couple told me that it was the whole question of the wife wearing a head covering that finally made them leave. At one point, the wife had bluntly asked the church elders if they con-

---

* A significant number of those interviewed were adjusting to new forms of worship and their comments comparing and contrasting their worship experience are recorded in Appendix A under "Lack of Vitality."

sidered her to be less spiritual because she did not wear a head covering. Their answer was an emphatic yes. This hypocrisy upset her because she knew many of the women who wore head coverings were not very spiritual or even submissive to their husbands. This was the final straw for this couple so they left the assembly.

This hypocrisy affected many women deeply— especially in the worship service. A key distinctive of the Brethren is the reputed emphasis on the priesthood of all believers. But in practice, this works out to be the priesthood of male believers only. Women in the assemblies sit week after week listening to the same few men share and pray. Any young, immature man is free to get up and share the most superficial witness, while women, regardless of their spiritual maturity, their knowledge of the Word and their spiritual gifts, are not allowed to participate.

Many see this as inconsistency. A former missionary who is currently a commended worker in the Chicago area relayed this extremely relevant story about her relationship with an elder and his wife:

> I had grown to love them very much. He was 90, had terminal cancer, and she was not well. They were unable to get out to any of the meetings. On a number of occasions I would call up and say, "I've got a pie. Can I bring it over?" He loved rhubarb pie and one particular evening I took them a hot one. We made tea and the wife got out the ice cream and good dishes. For two hours the three of us sat around the kitchen table reminiscing about how good God has been in our lives. It was a beautiful time of genuine fellowship around the Lord. When we were all through, he thanked me profusely for coming and cheering up what otherwise would have been a dull evening.

> As I was leaving, I said, "Tom, it has been a joy for me to be here. I have loved it, but I want to ask you something. Suppose that instead of having a rhubarb pie on the table tonight, we had had a loaf of bread, and instead of having a pot of tea, we had had a cup of wine. And suppose in that fourth chair over there the Lord Jesus Himself came in and sat down at this table. Do you really think He would have turned to Betty and me and said, Now, you two women shut up and go fetch something and put it on your head as a symbol of your shutting up? Do you really think that would have happened?"

> The old fellow shook his head, his eyes flooded with tears, and he said, "I do not believe that. We have really wronged you women all down through the years. You will just have to forgive us . . ."

> This was a moment of truth for him.

Parochialism

A final source of disaffection with the Brethren assemblies is the parochialism or provincialism found there. Those with limited perspectives or who are narrowly sectarian in their thinking describe too many in the church who hold dogmatically to certain beliefs and practices.

Although few of those questioned listed parochialism as the main reason for leaving the Plymouth Brethren, yet almost everyone mentioned it as a contributing factor. In fact, as they reflected further and became exposed to the broader Body of Christ, their earlier parochialism loomed as a major source of disaffection and became the single area which generated the most anger and resentment.

But not only those who have left the Brethren have a parochialism story to tell; many leaders currently within the movement also feel the pain of parochialism. Because this problem is so widespread, this criticism, no matter how severe, needs to be carefully evaluated, not feared. If the principles we believe are true, they will stand the most intense form of scrutiny. If the principles are not biblical or if our application of them is faulty, then we can only lose if we do not seriously listen to our critics.

The interviews with those who had left the Brethren began to point out that once people had begun to do in-depth comparisons, the road back to the Brethren became extremely difficult. One typical commentator said,

> When we moved away from the Brethren, it was a tentative move at first. We were sort of testing the waters. But when we got involved in another church, we felt so liberated that we did not realize how frustrated we were until we got out and looked back at the situation... We became frustrated over the provincialism of the Brethren... There was a whole Christian world out there that the Brethren had written off or ignored and we were being enriched by that world... The parochialism of the Brethren began to wear us down.

Another couple, third- and fourth-generation Brethren, who are now active in a denominational church commented:

> Our whole world revolved around our families and the assembly, which often were the same. For the first time in our Christian experience we are relating to non-Christians. It is very liberating.

Another said, "There was more to the Christian life than we were allowed to experience [in the assemblies]. Our broadening outlook caused us to be more frustrated."

Many who have come out of the Brethren movement express these feelings of having been restricted in their understanding and perspective. One third-generation ex-Brethren made this revealing statement, "My past affects me. That is the main reason we have not joined a church. I still feel guilty walking into a church with a denominational label." Another highly-educated ex-Brethren from a well-known Brethren family said rather incredibly, "It was not until late in my life that I began to have the notion that there were saved people outside the Brethren."*

Ex-Brethren not only assess their background as being narrow and restrictive, but also feel the Brethren were excessively dogmatic in what they believed and how they practiced their beliefs. One third-generation Brethren woman commented almost facetiously:

> The impression I gained in the Brethren was that we were a notch above all other Christians. We had the right truth. Others had the truth, but we had the *right* truth.

Another couple still in the Brethren said, "We were taught that other bodies of Christians were part of the sects and systems which was the religious Babylon."

The following story illustrates this dogmatism:

> I heard an Emmaus Bible School teacher say in our assembly two years ago that there are fewer than 1,000 churches in the whole of the United States of America where they know what true worship is. He went on to say that only in the assemblies do we know what true worship is.

The exclusivism and the arrogance of this stance was told us by a man, whom we will call George, who was in the process of leaving the Brethren and going to another church. His mother-in-law had asked his wife, "How does George feel about giving up his priesthood?"

George commented, "The interesting thing behind that statement is the idea that only those who worship the way we do can experience the priesthood of all believers."

Later when their young son developed a severe medical problem—rheumatoid arthritis—they were pained when in reference to the fact they had left the Brethren-fold, a relative said to them, "Maybe God is trying to tell you something."

---

* For further comments see Appendix A under "Parochialism."

George reflected on this cruel statement:

> Clearly it was not a well thought-out statement. It was not timely. Since it came from our own family, it was easier to forgive. But it is a very revealing statement. The Brethren have an arrogance about them. Most of the time it is an uninformed or ignorant arrogance, but nevertheless an arrogance. They have discovered or have been given *the* form of worship and anything outside that form somehow does not match up. So in God's sight, all others fail. When you boil that down, you have arrogance.

We began to ask our interviewees about the source of this uninformed arrogance? An ex-Brethren academician commented:

> Somehow the Brethren feel they have discovered first century worship and they have a mandate to duplicate that. This has become their distinctive and mission. This is uninformed arrogance and unintentional ignorance, but arrogance and ignorance nevertheless. It is arrogance and ignorance because no way is Brethren worship anywhere near first century worship and there is no clear-cut mandate to duplicate it in the twentieth century.

Under the rubric of parochialism we should mention the anti-education and anti-intellectual attitude mentioned by a large number of those interviewed. A former activist among the assemblies in Southern California said,

> There is very little honest critical thinking that goes on in the assemblies, largely because the larger population in the assemblies are of the blue collar people. I don't want to sound elitist, but it is a fact. Let me explain: Very few of our parents were college educated. A number of our generation are college educated. Almost all of our children are college educated. Yet the eldership, by and large, are still in our parents' generation. It is threatening to them. Therefore, education is suspect; critical thinking is suspect. You simply cannot challenge what is taught or done.

Especially the educated feel this anti-intellectualism.*

Interestingly, when a most influential full-time worker, who is also a leading elder of an assembly located right next door to a college campus, was asked what he would change if he could change anything in the assembly, responded, "I would move the assembly a mile away from the campus"! This rather disturbing

---

* Note further comments in Appendix A under "Parochialism."

answer showed how threatened he felt by the progressiveness of the college atmosphere.

The most insightful comment on parochialism came from a wise full-time worker from New England:

> I am inclined to think we have a spiritual problem more than any doctrinal problem. Our problem is spiritual pride. It is seen in an attitude that says we do not have anything to learn. It is seen in an attitude that is suspicious of anything that is new. It is seen in the attitude that insists that everyone must agree on every doctrine. It is seen in the attitude where we cannot tolerate differences. Really what this comes down to is a commentary on our own insecurities.

And so these sources of disaffection for those leaving the Plymouth Brethren assemblies have been categorized and their stories have been synthesized. It is not a complete story because all the areas touched on in the interviews were not discussed. Many brought up the lack of pastoral care as a contributing factor for leaving, others mentioned the lack of evangelism, and one full-time worker even connected the lack of evangelism to the parochialism of the assemblies:

> The assemblies that I have known since I was a boy have long since lost contact with the world. There is no contact with the non-Christian unless it is in your work. The only contact with a non-Christian that was considered legitimate was to bring them to church so that the gospel could be preached to them. This led to an extreme position of separation. There is an inhibition factor preventing outreach. Non-Christians are not seen as friends. Friendship with a nonbeliever was an absolute taboo. Therefore, very little personal evangelism happened.

The story of the disaffected is also incomplete because only a selected sampling of those leaving was taken. The vast majority of those leaving the church are not leaders and we opted to interview only 52 of those who were or are currently leaders. Although the picture they painted was bleak, so are the facts: people are leaving and the Plymouth Brethren tradition is in a declining situation in North America. Only as we grapple with these facts can we seek solutions and begin to revive our hope. We can make constructive moves to reverse this trend, even though, as the wag has it, "It is easier to deplore the malady than to prescribe the cure."

So we move now to putting our efforts at prescribing a cure. There is a great need to search the Scriptures and examine the principles underlying the purpose of the church. We must also search our own history to see how the original Brethren took the timeless and unchanging principles of the church and applied them to their time and culture. The time has come to examine critically and honestly our own traditions to see whether those timeless principles have suffered any distortion through the years. By honestly evaluating our local assembly to see where we stand in light of the principles of the Word of God, we can develop the courage to admit failure, confess our sins and plan for the future. There is hope if we do this and then begin praying and working for renewal.

In the words of an elder from a Northwest assembly:

There was a time that I thought the Brethren movement was dying on the vine. Now I think maybe there is hope, judging from some specific assemblies that I have either seen or heard about. Where assemblies are willing to launch out and to move into more imaginative directions, I think there is hope.

A Biblical Perspective of Church

8

The Apostle Paul has described God's master plan with clarity. It is "to bring all things in heaven and on earth together under one head, even Christ" (Ep 1:10). The means of accomplishing this is through the reconciliation that is in Christ. So, Paul states it is God's purpose through Christ "to reconcile to himself all things, whether things on earth or things in heaven, by making peace through his blood, shed on the cross" (Co 1:20).

Believers everywhere look forward to that day when God the Father will exalt God the Son and at the name of Jesus every knee shall bow and every tongue confess that Jesus Christ is Lord (Ph 1: 9-11). God the Holy Spirit will lead that great cosmic confession (1 Co 12:3b). It is mind boggling when one begins to contemplate the scope of the redemption that is in Christ. Even the physical universe will be part of the cosmic redemption (Rm 8:14-22). Every fractured result of the fall will be partially corrected by the redemptive power of the atonement (1 Co 1:30).

As mind boggling as this cosmic plan may be, it is equally humbling to realize that God has chosen the church to be part of that redemptive process. Not only are we the recipients of redemption that is in Christ, we are also the agents of that redemption and reconciliation.

To be sure, it was solely the work of Christ that redeemed and reconciled us to God. He is the one who made Jew and Gentile into one new person and presented them as one body to God (Ep 2: 14-16). He is the one who has taken us and placed us in Christ and made us one with all other believers.

> There is one body and one Spirit—just as you were called to one
> hope when you were called—one Lord, one faith, one baptism, one
> God and Father of all (Ep 4:4-6).

God has created this unity through Christ and he has given us the
responsibility of maintaining that unity. Paul states that the redeemed
are "to live a life worthy of the calling you have received. . . . Make
every effort to keep the unity of the Spirit" (Ep 4:1-3).

Even more than maintaining the results of reconciliation, the
church is to be a proclaimer and agent of reconciliation. Paul
stresses that it is through the church that the manifold wisdom of
God (his reconciling process) should be made known to the rulers
and authorities in the heavenly realms (Ep 3:10). It is through the
church that the message of reconciliation is taken to the world (2 Co 5:
18-20). It is in the church that reconciliation is to be practiced. So
the epistles of Paul, Peter and John exhorted believers to be reconciled to one another, to walk in love and to love one another as
Christ loved them.

This continuing experience of reconciliation allows Jesus to say
to those who followed him, "All people will know that you are my
disciples if you love one another" (Jn 13:35). Reconciliation becomes
the basis of Jesus' prayer, "That all of them may be one, Father, just
as you are in me and I am in you. May they also be in us so that the
world may believe that you have sent me" (Jn 17:21).

The ultimate apologetic to the world of nonbelievers is the love
and unity seen in the church of Christ. Unfortunately the body is
tragically divided today. It reminds one of a parody of the famous
line in a hymn, "Like a mighty army moves the church of God":

> Like a herd of turtles moves the church of God; brothers, we are
> treading where we've always trod. We are all divided, many bodies
> we; very strong on doctrine, weak on charity (Watson 1979:95).

But no matter how divided and weak we may be, we are still part
of God's master plan because we are part of his redeemed community known as the church. Thus the imperative to look more
closely at the nature and purpose of this unique phenomenon
called the church.

Paul Minear states, "The New Testament idea of the church is
not so much a technical doctrine as a gallery of pictures" (1972:617).
This interesting observation if correct, could help explain why
there is so much controversy among different church traditions

over which doctrine of the church is correct. Could it be that the New Testament does not give us a totally developed theology of church structure? Could it be that God never intended the New Testament to be read as a textbook on church truth?

Although these questions go beyond the scope of this study, still F. F. Bruce points out that these were the kinds of questions Henry Craik was dealing with at the inception of the Brethren movement and that they need to be reexamined in the light of the New Testament (1979:158-159).

Secondly, Minear's comment about the church being a gallery of pictures relates particularly to metaphors and images of the church. In such figures one can see the purpose of the church revealed, for in almost every metaphor and image there is an essential element illustrating a living and loving relationship between Christ and the church.

The Church as the Temple of God

The church as God's temple stresses the worshiping aspect of God's community. The temple was a place where the people of God came to worship Jehovah. Peter states:

> As you come to him, the living Stone . . . you also, like living stones, are being built into a spiritual house to be a holy priesthood, offering spiritual sacrifices acceptable to God through Jesus Christ (I P 2:4-5).

Spiritual sacrifices would include giving to God the praise and adoration and worship that is his due.

This metaphor carries with it three specific applications: First, the individual believer is to realize that one's physical body is a temple of God. The spiritual life of that temple is given by God through the Holy Spirit who resides in the soul of each genuine believer. This is truth beyond our comprehension but not beyond our experience. This truth, so universally applied yet so individually experienced, is one of the great mysteries of our faith. George Mallone correctly states, "The breath of God and the image of God in [persons] mix as new ingredients in every believer" (1981:174). All believers are unique temples of God. This implies that each one would worship God through his own unique personality.

The implications of this can be tremendously liberating for we are thus free to worship God through the personality God has given us. No one is wired with the exact same emotions and intellect. Each person ought to be free to express their worship to God without being stifled in their soul.

Practically, this means that we should not feel discomfort when seated next to those who choose to close their eyes and lift up their hands while singing praises to God. Maybe I am too inhibited emotionally to do that, but who is to say that my emotions are the norm for everyone else? The reverse is equally true. The more expressive person should not be intimidated or made to feel uncomfortable by a quiet and more reflective kind of worshiper. Recognizing and accepting that everyone of us is a unique sanctuary of worship might enhance both our personal and collective worship.

A second application seen in the metaphor of a church being the temple of God relates to the local church. Paul says to the Corinthian church:

> Don't you know that you yourselves are God's temple and that God's spirit lives in you? If anyone destroys God's temple, God will destroy him; for God's temple is sacred, and you are that temple (1 Co 3:16-17).

Here the word for temple (that person) is the word *naos* which indicates the very place that God resides. When the local church gathers together, God, in a marvelous and unique way, resides in the midst of his people. Again, the residing presence of God is through the corporate indwelling of the Holy Spirit. In some mysterious way, God's presence is in the local temple. The temple, the local church, is sacred because it is where the people of God come to worship. Paul is warning the Corinthians in light of this sacred responsibility.

In context, the destructive potential comes from schisms. God has a particular hatred for those who divide and ruin the local church. Schism, in the New Testament church, was not caused so much by false teachers teaching erroneous doctrine but by willful groups dogmatically pursuing positions in disregard for the higher principle of unity. Note the words:

> For since there is jealousy and quarreling among you, are you not worldly? Are you not acting like mere men? For when one says, "I follow Paul" and another, "I follow Apollos," are you not mere men? (1 Co. 3:3-4).

Jesus' words remain true: "the gates of Hades will not overpower it" (the church), yet this must refer to the universal church composed of those who have made the great confession that Jesus is the Christ, the Son of the living God (Mt 16:16-18). Because the local church can be ruined and has been ruined many times by the sin of sectarianism. When a local church dies, the lamp stand is removed and in a mystical, yet actual, way the Holy Spirit's corporate presence is gone.

The word for spirit comes from the Greek word *pneuma* which means wind, breath or spirit. When the Spirit, or breath of God, is gone from the corporate temple of God, there is death in the local church. Having individual Christians indwelt by the Spirit of God does not guarantee that the local church will be experiencing the corporate presence of the Holy Spirit. Paul assumed the Corinthians were Christians (1 Co 1:2), which in turn presupposed the personal indwelling of the Holy Spirit (Rm 8:9). This being true, it was still possible for that church to be ruined. In fact, Paul stated that their worship (their coming together for the Lord's supper) was not for the better but for the worse and there was no way he could praise them in that situation (1 Co 11:17).

In light of Paul's warning here to the Corinthians and also to the Thessalonians about quenching the Holy Spirit (1 Th. 5:19), one would be wise to ponder the words of Dr. Carl Bates:

> If God were to take the Holy Spirit out of our midst today, about 95 percent of what we are doing in our churches would go on, and we would not know the difference (Watson, 1973:13).

Finally, the metaphor of the temple is applied to the universal church. With Jesus Christ as the chief cornerstone, "the whole building is joined together and rises to become a holy temple in the Lord . . . a dwelling in which God lives by his Spirit" (Ep 2:21-22). The entire church, the universal Body of Christ, is being joined together. Each stone is being placed into the temple in its proper place. Every stone has a specific place and function. The word for "rises" is the word *group*. This is an organic temple being built by living stones (1 P 2:5), each of which is being placed in order in relationship to the chief cornerstone, Jesus Christ.

This metaphor obviously points to the unity of the Body of Christ. We all belong in this temple. There is a spiritual unity that transcends all cultural, racial, economical, political and even biblical differences. In God's sight "there is one body and one spirit . . . one Lord, one faith, one baptism" (Ep 4:4-5).

How it must be a stench in the nostrils of God to see his people divided. It is claimed that there are now over 9,000 registered Christian denominations. What a tragic denial of the church being the temple of God. Jesus wept during his incarnation over the unbelief of Israel (Lk 19:41). He was grieved and distressed in the Garden of Gethsemane as he contemplated the cross (Mt 26:38). Today, what grief and distress must be his as he today regards the tragic condition of the temple of God, the church. May God grant us ears to hear what the Spirit is saying to us about our place in the temple of God.

The Church as the Household of God

The metaphor of the church as the household of God carries a number of profound ideas—the central picture being that of a family. We are a community of brothers and sisters in the family of God. Paul confirms this:

> I am writing you these instructions so that . . . you will know how people ought to conduct themselves in God's household, which is the church of the living God, the pillar and foundation of the truth (1 Tm 3:15).

He says elsewhere, "You are no longer foreigners and aliens, but fellow citizens with God's people and members of God's household" (Ep 2:19). The author of Hebrews confirms this truth, "Christ is faithful as a son over God's house. And we are his house" (Heb 2:6).

What does this mean to be a member of the household of God? What does it mean to be family? First, it means that we became family members by adoption and we are certified as legitimate children in the family of God through the reception of the Holy Spirit who in turn causes us to cry "Abba, Father" (Ga 4:5-6; Rm 8:14-16). Second, it means that those who call God Father we must call our brothers and sisters. Within the family of God there is a wide variety of people from all social classes (1 Co 1:26-27), yet all are one in Christ (Ga 3:28). Third, it means we have family responsibilities. Most of the epistles are written with these responsibilities in mind.

The primary characteristic that ought to govern the family of God is love. One of the clearest and most succinct passages detailing our family responsibility is found in Romans:

> Love must be sincere. . . . Be devoted to one another in [familial] love. Honor one another above yourselves. . . . Share with God's people who are in need. Practice hospitality (12:9-13).

Specifically our family responsibility means our love for one another must be sincere or without hypocrisy (Arndt et al 1957:76). This is a necessary admonition because Paul realized the propensity that the human heart has towards hypocrisy. The key to a healthy family, church or institution is good and honest communication within a bond of love. What makes a family healthy is the fact that each member is known, accepted and loved.

Often, however, the church has not been a community in which there is an atmosphere of family. Rather a fear of being known appears to dominate with the parallel conviction that if one were really known, then they would not be accepted. If not accepted, then they would not be loved. All a vicious circle which means that the need for love and acceptance causes church members to project false images, thus breeding insincerity and dishonesty in the household of God.

Dietrich Bonhoeffer, commenting on the admonition in James 5:16 to "confess your sins to one another," makes essentially the same point:

> The pious fellowship permits no one to be a sinner. So everybody must conceal [their] sin from [themselves] and from the fellowship. We dare not be sinners. Many Christians are unthinkably horrified when a real sinner is suddenly discovered among the righteous. So we remain alone with our sin, living in lies and hypocrisy. The fact is we are sinners (1954:110).

Paul, talking in a context about how Christians are to relate to one another says, "Therefore each of you must put off falsehood and speak truthfully to [their] neighbor, for we are all members of one body" (Ep 5:25). This implies that if there is dishonest communication in the church, the body suffers.

Dishonesty in the church often is not malicious or even intentional. It might come from one's concept of what it means to be spiritual, or from the many sermons heard, the biographies of great Christians that have been read, as well as the genuine examples of godly men and women. Often these sources have more shaping influence than the Word of God, yet it is helpful to study the scriptures where biblical characters are portrayed with ringing realism. The Bible quickly takes the air out of the super-spiritual balloon when we see through whom and how God has worked in times past.

There is a great need in the household of God to love one another sincerely. This practically means to walk honestly before God and our brothers and sisters while accepting and loving them as part of the family of God. It is a wonderful truth to know that God loves us and has accepted us in Christ. This truth, no matter how marvelous and true, has no feeling until it has actually been felt by the love and acceptance of those in the household of God.

The metaphor of the church as the household of God emphasizes fellowship and relationship within the community of believers and this was stressed by Anthony Norris Groves (1795-1853), one of the major ideologists of the movement that came to be known as the Plymouth Brethren.

The Church as the People of God

The church as the people of God is more than a metaphor— it is a powerful concept with roots deeply embedded in the Old Testament. Peter points out the connection of the church as the people of God to the Old Testament:

> But you [the church] are a chosen people, a royal priesthood, a holy nation, a people belonging to God, that you may declare the praises of him who called you out of darkness into his wonderful light. Once you were not a people, but now you are the people of God; once you had not received mercy, but now you have received mercy (1 P 2:9-10).

Although the New Testament church is unique to God's plan of the ages, it is not new in essence because there can only be one people of God. And the obvious point of the church being the people of God is that it is to be a witness. The church becomes a public declaration of what God does when we are called out of darkness into his wonderful light.

Other expressions of this obligation are wrapped up in the term "saints"— which conveys the New Testament concept of what it means to be the people of God. The saints of the New Testament refer to the whole people of God rather than to an elite group of special Christians who are noted for their outstanding piety. It also expresses the action of God rather than the moral quality of those who are called saints since they are those God has set apart to be his unique people, dedicated to worship, to fellowship and to being a witness in the world today.

Sanctification also expands the meaning of the concept of church as the people of God. There is a close lexical relationship between the title, saints, and the concept of sanctification. William Barclay points out that the root meaning of both is seen in the world:

When Paul calls the Christian *hagios* (saint), he means that the Christian is [one] who is different from [others] because [that person] specially belongs to God and to the service of God. And that difference is *not* to be marked by the withdrawal from ordinary life and activity, but by showing in ordinary life a difference of quality and character which will mark [this one] out as the [person] of God (1962:11-12).

This important concept emphasizes that to be the people of God means to bear the title of saint and to be one who is sanctified by being different in the world. Historically this truth has been distorted when well-intending Christians have emphasized the concept of separation from the world over the idea of being different in the world. The failure comes in misunderstanding Jesus' teaching on separation. Jesus taught and modeled the truth that those who follow him should separate themselves from sin. He never taught nor modeled that his followers should separate themselves from sinners. This kind of separation leads to isolation and tragically distorts the purpose of the church. When this happens, the church has failed to be the people of God in the world by hiding its lamp under a bowl (Mt 5:13).

So these three metaphors point out the purposes of the church: As the temple of God, the church is to be a worshiping community; as the household of God the church is to be a family in fellowship with each other; and as the people of God the church is to be a witnessing community in the world.

The most unique and complicated metaphor used of the church is that expressed by Paul as the Body of Christ. This is the only metaphor of the church that is not related in some way to the Old Testament, yet, it is complicated in that it deals with the many-faceted relationships between Christ and those who belong to him. The metaphor suggests that the structure of the church is to be understood organically rather than institutionally, while conveying the powerful idea that the church as the Body of Christ is a part of an ongoing incarnation.

The organic model seen in the metaphor of the Body of Christ is developed by Paul primarily in the book of Ephesians and Colossians (Ep 1:23; 4:12-16; 5:17-30; Col 1:18; 2:19). However, the practical outworking of the model is seen in 1 Corinthians 12:12-17 and Romans 12:3-8 where the common life of the church is described in terms of interdependence. The body is seen as a unit composed of many parts which must function together for normal health.

In the body analogy, the church functions through gifts (parts of the body) such as the gifts of leadership or enabling. Gifted leaders are given to the church "to prepare God's people for works of service so that the Body of Christ may be built up" (Ep 4:11-12). Individual members build the body by exercising the gifts God has given them. In Corinthians Paul warns us that no one should despise the contribution that other members are making to the organic structure nor should they consider their own contribution as insignificant (1 Co 12:12-27).

The practical implications of this are tremendous since it causes us to define the church organically rather than institutionally. It is interesting to note the reformational concept that came out of the International Congress on World Evangelism at Lausanne, Switzerland in 1974.

Martin Luther in 1530 stated the church is "the congregation of saints, in which the gospel is rightly taught and the sacraments rightly administered" (Bettenson 1947:298). To Luther the church was institutional— a repository where right belief, right teaching and right order existed. On the other hand, representatives from every evangelical group in the world at Lausanne signed a statement that said:

> The church is the community of God's people rather than an institution, and must not be identified with any particular culture, social or political system, or human ideology" (Douglas 1975:9).

This is a different perspective concerning the church. The church as the people of God is an organic rather than institutional structure. But in spite of the ringing affirmation given to the Lausanne statement it would seem that the reformational concept of the church as institution still has its influence today.

One attitude predominant in an institutional model church concerns success. The orientation becomes achieving specific objectives and the best way to do this is to organize institutionally. Therefore, the church assumes a hierarchical structure, delegates authority, and measurably sets goals to see if objectives are accomplished. Unfortunately, as a corollary, the institutional model produces impersonal relationships, formality, and a church characterized as a repository of convictions rather than a community of people.

The institutional model posits the church as a matrix from which right doctrine and right order is practiced. Larry Richards and

Clyde Hoeldtke argue in their *A Theology of Church Leadership* that the institutional model is unbiblical.

> Our view of the Body of Christ as an organism, in contrast to an organization or institution, has led to a radical rejection of many traditional church-leadership concepts. In particular those ideas that lead to the management or direction of the local church are suspect, for they seem to intrude on the role Jesus himself is called on to play as head of the church. This view is supported not only by a biblical understanding of the church as a living organism, but also by a biblical description of leadership (1981:206).

Howard Snyder also says:

> A certain degree of institutionalization is therefore inevitable and even desirable in the church. . . . It is sociologically naive to say the church is in no sense an institution. Any pattern of collective behavior which has become habitual or customary is already an institution. In the broad sense the Lord's supper is an institution; and even a small group Bible study, if it meets continually over a period of time, becomes an institution (1977:63).

When the church is viewed as an organism, the emphasis will be placed on interpersonal relationships, fellowship, interdependence and mutuality with the results being that the body will grow and build itself up in love, as each part does its work (Ep 4:16). As Richards and Hoeldtke say, "The first priority of an organism must always be the nurture, growth, and maturity of itself and its members (1981:195).

Thus the question church leaders must answer is, What model characterizes our congregations? Are they solely an institution or are they an organism, or perhaps even a combination of both? One simple test might be to ask church leaders what characterizes their own meetings. Are they mainly business meetings involving organizational goals? Are they relational so time is taken for nurturing the members? How much time is spent sharing specific needs and praying for one another? The elders form a microcosm of the church, so how they operate becomes vitally important to the life of the body.

Along with the metaphor of the church as the Body of Christ is the powerful idea that Christ is still with us in the world today—the corporate church being a loving Christ in our desperate world. David Watson connects this to the need for renewal and evangelism.

Unless renewal precedes evangelism, the credibility gap between what the church preaches and what the church is will be too wide to be bridged. It is only when the world sees the living Body of Christ on earth that it will be in any way convinced of the reality and relevance of Christ himself (1978:18).

The living Body of Christ on earth conveys the ongoing incarnation of Christ. To be sure, Jesus' incarnation was unique. There can be only one visitation of God as person within time and space. However, in a spiritual sense Christ is still alive incarnating the church, so Jesus prayed:

As you sent me into the world, I have sent them into the world . . . just as you are in me and I am in you . . . that they may be one as we are one: I in them and you in me (Jn 17:18-23).

Paul also said, "I have been crucified with Christ and I no longer live but Christ lives in me" (Ga 2:20). John tells us God promised that when Christ appears, "we shall be like him for we shall see him as he is" (I Jn 3:2). Yet, this is not the whole truth. Paul says God's transformation is now in process for we "are being transformed into his likeness with ever-increasing glory, which comes from the Lord, who is the Spirit" (2 Co 3:18).

Clearly the New Testament tells us we are all individually members of the Body of Christ, corporately we form a living organism. As part of that living body we are a contemporary expression of Jesus Christ in the world. As part of the ongoing incarnation, we are responsible for the mission of Jesus Christ.

To be effective in the ministry which Jesus began, we must be a vital part of the living Body of Christ. Nothing deadens more than proclaiming to be the Body of Christ while not practicing the mission of Christ. As was profoundly expressed in the Lambeth Conference paper:

If we preach the incarnation, then we must ourselves live by the principle of the incarnation, humbling ourselves as Christ humbled himself, serving as he served, renouncing affluence and cultivating a simple life-style, and identifying ourselves with the world in its pain.

If we preach the cross, then we must ourselves take up the cross and follow Christ, dying to our own self-centeredness in order to live for others, loving, forgiving and serving our enemies, and overcoming evil with good.

If we preach the resurrection then we must ourselves live in its power, experiencing deliverance from the bondage of sin and fear of death, and eagerly expecting the completion of the new creation when Christ returns.

If we preach the Ascension, then we must submit ourselves to the universal authority of the reigning Christ, longing that every tongue should confess him as Lord and that more and more of human society should come under his rule.

If we preach Pentecost, we must then ourselves demonstrate the power of the Holy Spirit in our lives, as he makes Christ in us and binds us together in love. If we preach the church as God's new and reconciled community, then we must set ourselves resolutely against the re-erection of racial, social and sexual barriers which Christ abolished (Ep 2:11; Ga 3:28), and must seek his grace to become the united, accepting, caring and supportive fellowship which he means us to be (1978).

The Lost Perspective

9

Though here we are not intending to give a comprehensive overview of what happened to the original Brethren renewal since that has been done effectively by many—including the detailed and accurate accounts of Rowdon (1967) and Coad (1968). It also would not be edifying to rehearse the specific issues or the many divisions which followed.

Rather what is needed is an interpretation of the renewal as well as the long-lasting effects it had upon the very principles which originally motivated the movement in the first place. The purpose of this overview for those genuinely interested in renewal is to give them a better understanding of the roots of this revival and the long-term effects it had on those it touched.

To use the new wine/old sacks imagery, the original Brethren made new wine but the older forms of the Anglican church and the dissenting churches could not contain it. New wineskins were needed and so the Brethren movement came into existence. This new life was expressed through creative forms of worship and service, but as always, raised when old forms of worship and service are rejected, the question becomes: What guides the new forms?

The original Brethren, for their part, answered "The Scriptures." But then the question becomes: Who interprets the Scriptures? Surely the Holy Spirit gives guidance, but who interprets this to the people of God? Usually it behooves the leaders of the movement to do this.

No one more powerfully influenced the early Brethren movement than John Nelson Darby, nor caused it to grow as much.
Darby also influenced the entire evangelical world in prophetic
matters and was obviously used of God. However, by the same
token, no one did more to retard and stifle a continuing experience
of renewal among those who came from the Brethren tradition. His
influence is still felt by those who are products of that tradition.

Although it is true that he became the acknowledged leader of
the narrower group which became known as the "Exclusive Brethren," still his influence has permeated the entire movement far
more than most are aware. A recent study indicated that the open
Brethren in America have their origins far more in the exclusive
wing of the church than in the open wing (McLaren 1982).

If this study is accurate then the obvious questions become: How
did Darby and exclusivism alter the original Brethren renewal and
what are the consequences of this?

Historical analyses would indicate that as interest in prophecy
intensified, John Darby began to put together a theological system
of thought. He was thoroughly convinced that the Anglican church
not only was in complete ruin and apostasy, but also that Scriptures
taught that all of Christendom was in ruin and an apostate condition.
The church (Christendom) had lost its unity and purity, along with
any power that it used to have. No longer was it capable of bearing
witness to God in their present world. The church's ministry had
become totally corrupt— the ordinances had become worldly and
the clergy had received their authority from persons and not from
God.

In Darby's view the Holy Spirit had been totally rejected as the
giver of gifts and the guide in worship. Therefore the entire nature
and purpose of the church had been so perverted that it had
become the opposite of what God had intended for it. Had Darby
stopped here, limiting his remarks only to his own experience in
the Anglican church, no one would have disagreed much. But he
went one step further and posited that the church could no longer
be restored. For Darby there could be no renewal because he was
thoroughly convinced that Scriptures taught that each "dispensation" ends in ruin and God never restores this dispensation.

Darby began to go farther out on the limb: He said the church
had failed, even in apostolic times. The apostles failed to fulfill the
great commission, which was evidence that the dispensational age
of the church was also failing. Though the church had fought apostasy

at first, slowly apostasy and evil began to be found within the church. Even the New Testament church had failed and came to utter ruin, yet the church could not be restored. Darby wrote:

> Has the church kept itself in this goodness of God? Truly Christendom has become completely corrupted; the dispensation of the Gentiles has been found unfaithful: can it be again restored? No: impossible. As the Jewish dispensation was cut off, the Christian dispensation will be also. May God give us grace to continue steadfast in our hope, and to rest upon His faithfulness, which will never fail us (1971 II:320-321).

Later he said:

> God has always begun by putting his creatures in a good position; but the creature invariably abandons the position in which God set it, becoming unfaithful therein. And God, after long forbearance, never reestablishes it in the position it fell from. It is not according to his ways to patch up a thing which has been spoiled; but he cuts it off, to introduce afterwards something entirely new and far better than what went before (1971 XIV:87).

So what are believers to do with its ruined church which cannot be renewed or restored? It was clear to Darby: They must withdraw from this evil and apostate church to become the remnant which Darby taught remained in every dispensation. This nucleus of uncontaminated Christian believers will be obedient to God and separate themselves from the evil system. These, then, would form circles of fellowship or assemblies of believers. Their responsibility would be to be faithful, to serve God and wait for the soon coming of Jesus Christ.

This form of "church truth" was preached on or written about from that time on by the more popular full-time Brethren workers. It also was a favorite theme of C. H. Mackintosh, (1966 III:45-46). McLaren in his study, traces this teaching throughout the early American Brethren pioneers (1982:35-45).

This belief about the church in ruins held tremendous implications for Darby. If the church is in ruin, so, too, are the offices of the church. The offices of elder and deacon are no longer valid because the power to activate the office no longer exists. Since there are no apostles today, elders and deacons— who are appointed by apostles— simply cannot exist.

How then is the church to function? Christ, the head of the

church, exercises his authority through the Holy Spirit. Those who separate from the ruined church and assemble in the name of the Lord Jesus form a unity through the Holy Spirit. Each local assembly is responsible therefore to Christ, the head, and to the Holy Spirit, the unifier. Where the Holy Spirit resides, there will be unity (Ep 4: 3). Assemblies are not bound together by law or creedal statements, but rather by mutual obedience to the Word of God and the continuing guidance of the Holy Spirit. The Spirit of God is to be in control, and if he is not, it is a denial of unity.

Darby also maintained this spiritual unity was to be a visible unity. The Body of Christ on earth is composed of individuals, so there is unity only of the whole. Each assembly must be attached to the whole which occurs when individuals place themselves on the ground of unity—found where two or three are gathered in his name (Mt 18:29). When this happens, the unity of the Spirit will be there.

Aligned to this question of unity is Darby's concept of evil. His pamphlet, "Separation from Evil—God's Principle of Unity," expresses his deep belief that the organized church was totally corrupt and full of evil. Only when a believer separated from that evil could unity be restored. He further developed this concept by positing two other manifestations of evil: personal and ecclesiastical.

Where personal evil involves moral sins, ecclesiastical evil occurs when the assembly abandons the true principles instituted by God and becomes preoccupied with human organization. Instituting elders and deacons or even prearranging ministry meetings would be an obvious preoccupation with human organization, thus a denial of the Holy Spirit's control and evil, so none of their meetings were to be prearranged. The ministry meeting was one in which the believers gathered to wait on the Spirit to lead one of the males to teach or preach. The breaking of bread likewise was to be a meeting in which the Holy Spirit was in control. With no format and nothing prepared, this would leave Christ, as the head of the body, free to exercise authority through the impulsive movement of the Holy Spirit.

John Darby's church in ruin doctrine was difficult for the average believer to understand, and few of the original Brethren ever did accept the church in ruin premise. The Bristol Brethren and Anthony Norris Groves, then in India, rejected in detail Darby's eschatology and ecclesiology.

F.F. Bruce observed:

Darby's eschatology and ecclesiology were interdependent elements in a carefully constructed system—not surprisingly, since in the New Testament itself eschatology and ecclesiology are interdependent. . . . It is plain, I think, that the "Brethren movement" was never a single movement proceeding in one direction. From the outset, there were two divergent tendencies which temporary circumstances brought together in what gave the superficial appearance of one movement. But when stresses and strains arose, the inconsistencies between these two tendencies became patent (Rowdon 1967:xii).

Although no one questions the fact that two distinct groups eventually emerged from the original Brethren movement, the overwhelming evidence indicates that both the Brethren movement, as well as the open Brethren in North America, have been influenced theologically and practically by the spirit of exclusivism (McLaren 1971). The consequences to the original Brethren renewal have been overwhelming, even to the present day.

The original Brethren, in a beautiful way, rediscovered what it meant to function as the temple of God, the household of God, the people of God and the Body of Christ. They allowed the church to be the church so that life and vitality permeated through them— individually and in their congregations. But as Darby's influence grew and the spirit of exclusivism spread, subtle changes began to occur and once again the reformed and revitalized church began to experience distortion. Something was wrong and signs of communal deterioration began to appear.

The Distorted Images

10

The image of the church as the temple of God unfortunately became distorted. "Meeting in the name of Jesus only" originally was a way of expressing one's identity with the whole Body of Christ, irrespective of denominational labels. The Lord's Supper was seen as a symbol of unity and the early Brethren engaged in corporate worship with all believers, conditioned only upon life in Christ. As Darby developed his theology of the church in ruin, as well as his concept of separation from evil, God's principle of unity—the Lord's Supper—became not a symbol of unity but more one of purity. Only those who had renounced ecclesiastical evil, the organized church, and agreed to meet as did the Brethren could claim to be in accord with the will of God.

The emphasis shifted from life to light, from practice to doctrine. The main concern became not a genuine belief but rather a total separation from one who acted on the light of the Word of God. Practically this meant that before any could partake of the elements at the worship meeting, they needed to be examined to see whether they had, in fact, separated themselves from evil. If they were tainted, damage could be done to the unity of the assembly because separatism is God's principle of unity. The worship service no longer was open to all, but only to those separated ones who held the right doctrine. In practice, it became more important to hold right doctrine than to have spiritual life. The shift was complete. Soon the expression, "We meet in the name of the Lord Jesus only," was as sectarian as saying, "We are Baptist," or, "We are members of the Anglican church."

This new understanding of church also affected other areas of the worship service. The original Brethren had excitedly involved themselves in new forms of worship— writing new music to fit new experiences* and experimenting with different forms within the worship service. Some services at this time were prearranged while others were more open giving them a sense of flexibility and freedom. So much so that controls had to be placed upon the worship in some places.

This all began to stop when Darby's view of the church forbade accepting any form of organization as originating from persons and not from God. Soon everything had to be scrutinized to determine whether it was in agreement with the truth. Church life began to be stifled, until finally a nonwritten method of worship evolved which turned out to be more inhibiting and more predictable than were prearranged services.

One observer at this time complained that there was a "vagueness and uncertainty about the worship" and "frequent, prolonged, freezing pauses." This person also noted that there was "a lack of teaching which was due in part to a scruple about preparing beforehand" which led to "a constant and extremely wearisome recurrence of favorite ideas" (Neatby 1901:92).

The shift from life to light and the transition from the Lord's Supper as a symbol of unity to a symbol of purity caused the Brethren to assemble around the "truth of remembering the Lord" rather than around the person and worth of the Lord Jesus. This subtle shift was to have long and lasting effects.

The image of the household of God was also being distorted. Among their own, original Brethren worked hard at intentional fellowship with all believers regardless of their social or economical status in life. This had proved to be a powerful testimony to the unity that they had as a practicing family. With respect to all believers, irrespective of titles and labels, the original Brethren also practiced the principle of inclusive unity with diversity. Being the family of God with this kind of acceptance and tolerance was an extremely attractive truth. Unfortunately, the spirit of exclusivism brought a halt to this inclusive practice.

---

* It is interesting to note the dates that the hymns still included in Brethren worship hymnals were written.

Admittedly, the original ecumenical acceptance of all based only upon a common life in Christ was idealistic, easier to state as principle than to practice. How much diversity is ever accepted within inclusive unity is always a debatable issue. So this difficulty played into Darby's concept of separation from evil itself as God's principle of unity. Unity was no longer seen as common life in Christ, but was based upon conformity to right doctrine. With unity by conformity the decree, gone was acceptance and tolerance and, in fact, tremendous pressure was felt to conform or not be accepted. It also meant everyone had to be scrutinized carefully for "a little leaven leavens the whole lump" (I Co 5:6).

With these dynamics existing in a fellowship, it was soon easy for the concept of family to become distorted. This also set into motion an unwritten and unspoken—yet powerful—need among the Brethren to be right. All truth became nonnegotiable. There was no ambiguity in the Word of God, so although sincere and godly believers could differ, one must be wrong. This heritage which permeated later generations of the Brethren had devastating results. The tendency was to separate rather than to compromise and division became a commonplace trait. Henry Ironside commented:

> It should be remembered that many Exclusive Brethren have through the years become discouraged and even disgusted with the bewildering divisions among themselves and have sought a way out by going in among the Open meetings. These have carried with them much that they had learned in their former associations and the result is that many Open meetings are now much more like Exclusive meetings than in past years (1941:143).

Unity by conformity and the need to be right distorted a beautiful principle of inclusive unity with diversity in the family of God. The ramifications of this distortion continue to this day.

A Distorted People

The original Brethren became the people of God because they witnessed to their world, making an impact upon their culture like few others have done. Their work with the poor and homeless caused a skeptical world to pause and consider the gospel they preached. They became the salt of the earth in England and Ireland.

Unfortunately, with the encroachment of exclusivism came the inevitable distortion of the image of the church as the people of God and eventually their witness became blunted as their testimony lost credibility. The emphasis upon separation caused the Brethren to separate themselves from sin but also from sinners and this led them to an isolationist stance. Coupled with this was a personal piety that emphasized one's heavenly calling almost to the exclusion of practical living. Believing the Lord's coming was imminent and that apostasy and evil were so dominant, they began to feel there was nothing much more to do but pray, "Come quickly, Lord Jesus."

This does not suggest that evangelism stopped, for the Brethren have always been evangelistic, but a definite shift did put the emphasis upon preaching the gospel and winning souls. The personal approach used by Jesus when he healed the sick and fed the hungry seemed to be dropped. Slowly the involvement with the poor, the homeless and the destitute alcoholic began to give way. All energies began to be directed toward more gospel meetings— with less results.

What the Brethren renewal movement experienced with regard to the poor is not unique to them. Almost every great renewal movement has gone through this same evolvement. A scholar once noted:

> One phase of the history of denominationalism reveals itself as the story of the religiously neglected poor, who fashion a new type of Christianity which corresponds to their distinctive needs, who rise in the economic scale under the influence of religious discipline, and who, in the midst of a freshly acquired cultural respectability, neglect the new poor succeeding them on the lower plane. This pattern recurs with remarkable regularity in the history of Christianity (Niebuhr 1957:34).

As renewal movements reach the poor, they sooner or later become upwardly mobile. At this point their congregations become middle class— and self-satisfied with their new status. The result is a status quo congregation. In such congregations the emphasis will be on preaching the gospel, but little effort will be made to meet the real needs of the less fortunate in their community. The tendency then becomes to congregate around those of like values, both spiritually and economically. Unity is formed around sameness and the assembly has gained respectability but lost its witness as salt. At this point the congregation has lost its perspective and its focus.

The church is pictured as the Body of Christ because there resides life. This organic life was evident in the original Brethren—

alive worshiping, witnessing and being the family of God with vitality and exuberance.

However, when Darby introduced his unique concept of the church, a shift began to take place. Rather than emphasizing life, the stress was upon light (Darby's term for understanding the church in ruin). Right doctrine became more important than being alive to God because in Darby's view one could not be fully alive until they had separated from evil. This evil included the organized church in whatever form it might be found. Obedience to Christ demanded separation.

Darby's intent was good. He wanted Christ to have his rightful place of authority over his body and as head of the body Christ ought to be its only authority. At this point, Darby, as most biblical scholars have, faced a difficult question: How does a resurrected, heavenly Christ direct a literal earthly body? Based upon his doctrine of the church in ruin, Darby concluded that Christ as the head of the body exercises direct control through the Holy Spirit. Anything organized by persons could not be of the Spirit of God.

The consequences were in the long run devastating. The offices of elders and deacons were for the apostolic church which was in ruins. There was no possibility of restoring it since, according to Darby, God never renews a dispensation that has failed. How then, practically, was the assembly to function? To Darby, the answer was obvious: The Holy Spirit would lead and provide spiritual gifts. As long as there were powerful leaders such as Darby around to help discern the Spirit's direction, the church functioned fairly well. But when these charismatic leaders, who were biblically well educated, began to pass from the scene, grave problems began to develop.

The subtlety of this dilemma is centered on the fact that Darby had uncovered a tremendous truth: All believers are gifted, all have functions and all have a place of service in the Body of Christ. There is no difference in status in the Body of Christ for all are priests before God. This foundational truth remains unquestionable. The distortion comes, however, when no distinction is made between the truth of the priesthood of all believers and ministry of the church.

Even though Scriptures clearly state that all believers are gifted, it is also clear that certain gifts which are more visible and public are leadership gifts given to the church for the equipping of the saints (Ep 4:11-12). Problems developed when the concept of the believer priesthood was blurred with the public ministry gifts so that it was determined that every male church member should have his turn on the platform preaching or ministering at the Lord's Supper. This distorted all the gifts. The verbal and high visibility gifts were valued above all the others. This was complicated by two other factors.

There was a tendency to confuse the exercise of spiritual gifts with spirituality so that the more one exercised public gifts at either the ministry meeting or at the breaking of bread meeting, the more spiritual they were thought to be— denying the biblical principle that spirituality is intricately connected with the fruits of the Spirit. The fruits of the Spirit spring from within one's character and have little to do with one's spiritual gift. Every believer in Christ has the opportunity to be spiritual although not every believer is equally gifted. The confusion resulting from this misconception has produced problems.

Another complication in regards to spiritual gifts was related to their exercise and to the leading of the Holy Spirit. Any prearrangement and advanced preparation was considered a practical denial of the Holy Spirit's leading. Thus spontaneity was encouraged and impulsive leading was expected. Normally the Brethren would gather for Bible readings and ministry meetings but no one would know who would open up the Word. Coming together they would wait on the Spirit's leading. Although historically this practice has been dropped by most, the exception remains at the breaking of bread meeting where spontaneity and open participation under the guidance of the Holy Spirit are still practiced. The subjective element of determining the Holy Spirit's leading remains a problem, even to this day.

Coupled with the conviction against prearrangement and personal preparation was a prejudice against any religious or biblical education— which, again, was seen as a denial of the Holy Spirit who was to be the teacher rather than humanly ordained institutions, and especially any institutions that sprang from the Anglican church. The ironic fact here was that almost all the early Brethren leaders had been trained in those institutions— some as top-rated scholars. Darby's separation from ecclesiastical evil stance had these concurrent antischolastic effects.

Another factor that must be remembered is that the majority of the early Brethren leaders were deeply concerned that Jesus would come back in their lifetime. Darby even predicted in a paper he wrote while in Switzerland that Jesus would return in the year 1842 (Coad 1962:118). Believing this to be true, the urgency of the moment made continuing education, especially in religious subjects, unnecessary, as well as compromising with ecclesiastical evil. This is not to say the Brethren were anti-education. As a whole they have valued education; however, religious education—no matter how theologically orthodox it might be—has always been viewed with suspicion. The effects of this are still being felt today.

One final consequence of this stand affected the offices of the church. Since the church-in-ruin doctrine eliminated any possibility for elders and deacons in the local assembly, the question became how practically business matters and legal questions, let alone spiritual matters, would be decided when there was no organized, responsible group or leader.

When decisions were needed, generally speaking special meetings were called, open for males who were concerned about the affairs of the assembly to come together in what were called simply "men's meetings" or "business meetings." The decision-making process followed the principle of unanimity. If the Holy Spirit was in control, there would be unity. Unfortunately, when this principle is applied to difficult questions concerning discipline and doctrinal issues, confusion reigns.

Eventually, a pattern developed. Because there were no elders, the assembly was led by default so that the more verbal and forceful personalities emerged as the actual leaders. Sometimes the assembly would be run by a gerontocracy—not by biblical eldership but rather rule by longevity. Those males who had been there longest and had been the most faithful in attendance became the real assembly decision makers. Unfortunately, this practice has affected not only the early Brethren who functioned without elders, but also present day assemblies who function with elders.

It should be noted that Darby and the influence of exclusivism did not go unchallenged by the early Brethren. His concept of separation was forcefully challenged by Anthony Norris Groves who in a lengthy letter to Darby in 1836 stated, "I would infinitely rather bear with all their evils than to separate from their good (Coad 1968:289).

Darby's long-time friend and fellow worker, Charles Hargrove, took exception to his concept of freedom of ministry and the spontaneous use of spiritual gifts. Hargrove wanted to counter the abuses that had begun to emerge and he wanted to see more control and less freedom in the public meetings. He stressed that those who minister should be the ones who have been acknowledged with the ability to edify. Ministry should be limited to those to whom God has given a public gift. He explained "that this was not a matter of education or ordination, but simply of proven ability from God witnessed to in the consciences of those who were spiritual (Rowdon 1967:229).

Concerning Darby's idea about eldership and organization being a sign of ecclesiastical evil, Groves said:

> For myself I would join no church permanently that had not some constituted rule. I have seen enough of that plan, of everyone doing what is right in [their] own eyes, and then calling it the Spirit's order, to feel assured it is a delusion (Coad 1968:128).

Darby's personal magnetism and popularity, however, won the day and so the Brethren movement has been indelibly stamped by him. To be sure, the church, as seen in the image of the Body of Christ, is still here today. Unfortunately, that image is no longer as clear as it was for the original Brethren from Plymouth, Dublin and Bristol. The Brethren renewal movement may not be as significant as other reform movements in the church, but it must be admitted that few renewal movements have grappled with more almost-forgotten truths than did these Brethren from Plymouth, Dublin and Bristol.

Few movements have done more to awaken the sleeping laity, or regain the vision for making worship the heart of the church and the secret for continuing renewal. It was they who told the laity of their privilege to worship as priests before God, while at the same time seriously caring for the poor and nurturing the physical needs of the body, irrespective of one's social standing.

So church historians acknowledge that the Brethren captured a truth about the Body of Christ—a spiritually alive organism, not simply an institution. By awakening the broader Body of Christ to their responsibility as functional priests serving God with their unique spiritual gift, this movement has amazed students of history who are impressed because the very principles of renewal that keep surfacing everywhere are not only biblical, but are also those that the early Brethren experienced. God is consistent in bringing the faithful remnant—like those who are connected historically and traditionally to the original Brethren—into continual renewal.

Regaining the Biblical Perspective

11

The original Brethren from Plymouth, Dublin and Bristol rediscovered principles of life for the church. They saw the church as a spiritually alive organism—the living Body of Christ—and experienced the reality of a living body. Unfortunately, this renewal became distorted by one of the original architects, John Nelson Darby.

The question now is, how might those congregations from the Plymouth Brethren tradition regain a biblical perspective of the local church, recapturing the original vision of the early Brethren? I would posit that there are three fundamental concepts that must be understood before renewal will again occur among the Brethren.

The Relationship Between Church Purpose and Structure

If, as we have said earlier, the purpose of the church is to be a worshiping community, it must be dedicated to nurturing itself as family while being a witness to the saving love of God in the world. In some spiritual, even mystical, way, the church is Christ's body today. But as the apostle on the Damascus road was asked, "Saul, Saul, why do you persecute me?" so we, too, hear the same question. It behooves us to ask as Saul did, "Who are you, Lord?" Christ answered him on that day, "I am Jesus, whom you are persecuting" (Ac 9:4-5). So it is, whenever in some mysterious way the church, the Body of Christ, is attacked, Jesus feels personally persecuted. Thus Paul later can say:

Now I rejoice in what was suffered for you, and I fill up in my flesh what is still lacking in regard to Christ's afflictions, for the sake of his body, which is the church (Col 1:24).

Again, in this personal way, Paul saw his suffering to be part of Christ's.

Since we are spiritually and organically Christ on earth today, we can extrapolate these foundational truths and discover the implications for the local church today.

The Difference Between Principle and Practice

Defining the principles of the local church is one of the most important tasks the leadership in the local church faces today. It would seem that the following list of principles were taught in the New Testament:

1. *The centrality of Jesus Christ.* Obedient love for the Lord is the basic characteristic of a truly Christian congregation.

2. *The unity of the Body of Christ.* Since the Lord forms the church, local fellowships ought to welcome gladly all whom he has brought into his fellowship. They ought also to seek ways to express their oneness with other Christian churches in order to be his witness to the world (John 17).

3. *The freedom of the Spirit.* The Holy Spirit is Christ's Vicar in the church. He should be allowed to lead congregations to develop new forms and methods of church life to express biblical principles and accomplish biblical purposes.

4. *The regular gathering of the congregation.* The congregation is called to worship God in all its corporate functions; to hear the Word of God and to respond to God in prayer; to observe the church ordinances of baptism (the mark of discipleship); and the Lord's Supper (the focus of worship); to send God's people into the world to represent him by meeting physical and spiritual needs.

5. *The development of congregational ministry.* The local church is the God-designed means to discover, develop and encourage the use of the God-given abilities of all persons in the congregation.

6. *The practice of discipline.* None of us live as an island for we belong to the Lord and to each other. Leadership and membership in the fellowship are responsible for the instruction, growth and loving correction of each member.

7. *The plurality of leadership.* The congregation is called to follow the guidance of qualified elders and deacons who are sensitive to the conditions and needs of the church.

8. *The responsible autonomy of each congregation.* Each church carries a primary responsibility to the Risen Head and a secondary responsibility to other congregations. We, as churches, are not independent but interdependent.*

These New Testament principles are binding on the church, not optional. To the degree they are followed, to that degree the church is New Testament. The converse is equally true for the local church which fails to follow these principles fails to be a New Testament church.

Always, care must be taken not to confuse principle with practice. For example, to assume that the way the Word of God is preached currently in our local churches was the exact way it was practiced in the New Testament times fails to understand the difference between principle and practice. The principle is to preach God's Word. The actual method of preaching is a matter of freedom and so we cannot make methodology the principle when it is but the servant of the principle.

This is equally true of worship. The principle of the Lord's Supper is worship. The methodology again is the vehicle of the principle. But confusing methodology with principle, we produce deadening results. To worship the Lord by observing the Lord's Supper means to consider the person and work of Jesus Christ, his life and death, his resurrection and coming again, praising and worshiping God in the partaking of the bread and wine.

On the other hand, when methodology is confused with principle, the emphasis shifts from worship to the way one worships. And again, confusion sets in when the practice of our current worship is assumed to be the New Testament pattern. If this is so, any deviation is taken as a violation of the New Testament. By confusing method and principle, we thus distort worship and create a mind set that says, in essence, that our form of worship is correct while all others are wrong. Where worship is seen rather as a principle, we have the basis for unity with all others who love and worship the Lord Jesus Christ.

---

* These New Testament principles of the local church have been formulated by the faculty of the California Center for Biblical Studies.

The Difference Between Loyalty and Conformity

The local church, as the Body of Christ, comes to realize that they are individually members of one another (Rm 12:5) and there is nothing they can do to change that fact (1 Co 12:12-27). There is a relational force or a centripetal force that pulls them together— namely the New Testament truth that we are one in Christ and that we are to be characterized by unity (Ep 4:1-6). The practical out-working of relational forces is a mutual loyalty based upon an acceptance of one another that comes from a nonjudgmental attitude toward each other. Relational forces create loyalty based upon the biblical principle of unity in diversity. Interestingly, every major passage on the spiritual gifts stresses this point (1 Co 12; Rm 12; Ep 4).

On the other hand, when the church is seen primarily as an institution, the relational force is rather a social force of conformity. This, unfortunately, is centrifugal in nature— forcing people apart. Richards and Hoeldtke describe the effects of two people within an institutional church:

> Bill and Carol are real people. Both are in churches that have deve-
> loped institutional life-styles and maintain institutional loyalty by
> pressing for conformity to their pattern of life. In each church the
> acceptable member (1) is quiet and obedient to the leadership; (2)
> fits into well-defined institutional roles; (3) is identified by *what* he
> or she believes; (4) maintains a comfortable, impersonal distance
> from others; (5) does not express personal problems; (6) attends a
> defined number of church functions; and (7) refrains from certain
> kinds of behavior, such as drinking wine. In each case conformity is
> enforced through a quiet but all-pervasive social pressure that unof-
> ficially expresses disapproval and lack of acceptance (1981:
> 214-215).

These constraints are realities that tremendously affect the congregation of God's people. Thus it becomes a spiritual imperative for the leaders in the church to understand clearly the purpose and structure of the local church.

Although it is incredible that God has included weak humanity in his cosmic plan of redemption, and even though historically humans have only produced a divided and anemic church, still they are, nevertheless, involved in accomplishing God's ultimate purpose of "bringing all things in heaven and on earth together under one head, even Christ" (Ep 1:10).

As part of God's master plan, it is important that the church remembers how it fits into time and space. God has called us to be his temple and the universal church is a temple which owns Jesus Christ as its head. In the same vein each individual congregation is a local temple of worship which the Holy Spirit indwells in a unique way. Individually, we are to worship God through the personalities God has given us.

God has also called us to be his household and we belong to the family of God. With this great privilege comes responsibility: We are to love the family of God in an accepting and honest way so that "we in all things may grow up into him who is the head, that is Christ" (Ep 4:15). Beyond this, God has called us to be his unique people—in the world as a different people, witnessing through our lives the saving purpose of God.

Structurally, the church is not an institution—it is a living organism known as the Body of Christ. This is not to say that the church doesn't have clear institutional form. Rather the church, as the organically living Body of Christ, has organic goals that must take priority over institutional goals. As F.F. Bruce states:

> The church is the dwelling-place of the Spirit, and "where the Spirit of the Lord is, there is freedom" (2 Co 3:17). Structures of ministry, government and order are of value so long as they provide vehicles for the free moving of the Spirit; when they cease to do that, they should be replaced by more suitable ones. Whatever at any time helps the church to discharge [its] proper functions—the worship of God, the strengthening of fellowship within [its] membership and the witness of outgoing and self-giving love to [humankind]— that is what matters. When the church thinks more of [its] status than of [its] service, [it] has taken the wrong path and must immediately retrace [its] steps. As the church's Lord was (and remains) the Man for others, the church must be the society for others, the community of the reconciled which is at the same time the instrument by which the reconciling grace of God in Christ is communicated to the world. All that enables the church to be this is true development; all that hinders the church from being this is departure (Ellis & Gasque 1979:168).

Applying the Biblical Perspective

12

The present-day need for renewal among congregations from the Plymouth Brethren tradition is obvious— from the dwin dling numbers and dying churches. The two surveys referred to in Chapter 6, conducted by International Teams and Lois Fleming, unfortunately substantiate this suspicion rather convincingly. Although neither surveys dealt with the reasons why people are leaving the church, our own analytical inductive survey uncovered these— which are also painfully recorded in Chapter 7.

So the question before us now is absolutely essential: How can the biblical principles and models discussed earlier be applied to our current situation? Renewal must always begin at the microcosmic level— not the macro. The Brethren movement will not be renewed until individual congregations seek, by God's grace and mercy, to do something about their improverished spiritual condition. Since a large portion of the assemblies are satisfied with their situation, they will most likely not be interested in renewal. For these congregations we merely pray and trust that the Lord will awaken them in his time. If they will not be awakened and continue their current course, they then should be allowed to die with dignity and grace. For the congregations open to change and renewal, there is hope. With these it is possible to engage in an honest and open evaluation of where they are headed and based on that, determine what strategy that might enhance renewal.

Evaluating the Local Church

A number of methods can be used to evaluate the local congregation. Professional church-consulting organizations exist that will contract with the local church for this purpose. They normally evaluate the church through questionnaires and personal interviews both with the leadership and key members of the congregation. Some of these consultants also do extensive demographic surveys of the community to determine the growth potential in the neighborhood. These conclusions are normally presented to the church leadership who must then take the ball from there. Some consultants have follow-up programs available to help the church develop new areas of ministry or else enhance programs already in place. One such organization doing an effective job is called "Churches Alive."

The advantages of using an outside consulting agency include allowing highly qualified specialists who bring a degree of objectivity, usually impossible for insiders, to help a church make what can be tough decisions as well as provide follow-up consulting for these suggested programs. By the same token, disadvantages exist. They are expensive and are unfamiliar with the local church as well as with the forceful Plymouth Brethren tradition. Thus consultants often have difficulty in objectively evaluating the Breaking of Bread service because they are not aware of all the unwritten assumptions that govern most assemblies which come straight from that tradition. Also, most consulting agencies are geared for working with small clergy-oriented churches so their follow-up strategies are also programmed for this. Of course, they often can modify their method and be effective in their task if they can successfully detect the underlying causes of those problems which arise from the unwritten traditions and assumptions. Assemblies which take advantage of these consulting agencies may find them initially very helpful and their follow-up programs very enriching; however, for long term success the root causes must be discovered and the history that gave birth to those unwritten, powerful assumptions that continue to govern the assemblies must be understood.

A detailed questionnaire for congregations that come from the Plymouth Brethren tradition is exhibited here (see Appendix B). Designed so the responses could be analyzed by a computer, the questionnaire evaluates six specific areas and collects a body of general information. Before using the questionnaire, it is best to share it with the leadership to see if they have any additional areas they would like evaluated. The administrators of the questionnaire are helped if time to address the whole congregation and give an orientation on how to write a good and helpful evaluation is given them.

From this exercise a lot of information about the health of the assembly can be revealed. For instance, the size of the group plus its longevity in attendance tells a great deal about the growth in the assembly. The distance people travel to attend the assembly also helps predict how attendance may be affected as demographic pressures increase. The general information also gives necessary data concerning attendance at the regularly scheduled meetings. A computer can analyze the attendance frequency of each age group and project probable future patterns.

The questionnaire included here has as a specific goal the evaluation of the leadership's and the congregation's goals. Do they have a clear concept of their goals and where they are going? Is there a feeling that the assembly is moving towards accomplishing those goals? These vital questions of direction need to be asked and evaluated.

Then there are related questions concerning communication. Is communication good between the leaders and the congregation? Does the congregation feel listened to and heard? How do elders regard change? How do the leaders and the congregation perceive having a full-time worker or administrator? How does the leadership respond to shepherding? Do the sheep really feel cared for? Are the elders approachable when one has personal problems? How does the assembly view itself in relation to the broader Body of Christ? Should they cooperate with other evangelical churches in political and social issues? What joint cooperation in evangelism exists?

Such questions provide a picture of the situation in the local assembly.

A second area of evaluation is the worship service. Scrutinizing the Lord's Supper is difficult because of the unwritten assumptions controlling its practice. If worship is central to renewal, then it must be looked at biblically and critically. So the questions are— what is the purpose of the Lord's Supper and what methods of remembering the Lord are used? The role of women in worship must also be examined. Here, too, computers can be used to analyze the various subgroups and how they respond to the worship meeting. How do regular and the occasional attenders at worship view the meeting? How do the attitudes of those who have attended for a short period of time compare with those who have a long history with the Brethren? This information becomes extremely helpful when implementing a strategy of renewal in worship.

This questionnaire also covers areas of assembly life. The pulpit ministry— or as it is often called the Family Bible Hour— is an extremely important part of the assembly, and so questions concerning its purpose and nature reveal whether this meeting is perceived primarily as an outreach meeting in which the gospel should be preached, or as a meeting where the whole counsel of God is preached and directed primarily toward Christians. At this point, fundamental questions concerning the philosophy of ministry need to be discussed in light of God's Word. Other questions probe the program and methodology of the church to see whether they detract or enhance the pulpit ministry.

The midweek meeting is another area to be evaluated because this is the meeting which is suffering a real drop in attendance. Hard questions need to evaluate the purpose of these meetings. Why are people not attending? What needs are not being met? The questionnaire will help the leadership understand the problems which should thus help them implement a strategy of renewal. The issue of fellowship climate needs also to be examined. What is meant by this is, what does it feel like in this assembly? What is the atmosphere in this fellowship like? Does one have to be related by marriage to feel at home in this assembly? Are people who are different accepted?

Finally, the questions of budget and finances need to be raised. The relative health of an assembly can often be seen in the budget. How much is earmarked for foreign missions often tells a lot about a fellowship's spiritual condition. How much is spent on home missions and evangelism will also give an indication of how much outreach is in fact being practiced. An expenditure report by program or by biblical activities will quickly tell one where the priorities are. The amount spent on pastoral work will indicate how important personal problems are to the leadership. If an assembly supports a full-time worker, it usually indicates a high quality of ministry and Christian education in that local assembly. Thus budget evaluation reveals a great deal, "For where your treasure is, there your heart will be also" (Mt 6:21).

Strategizing for Renewal

Once the local assembly has undergone this careful and prayerful evaluation, then the next step is to develop a strategy for renewal.

Although the evaluation process might cause one to appear a critic and constant evaluation tends to produce a critical and cynical spirit, still on the other hand one who tries to apply biblical principles can become an idealist. Idealism, when stifled enough times by reality, can lead to disillusionment, cynicism or bitterness. By God's grace, those who keep the goal of renewal ever before them will escape these tendencies.

If renewal is to be authentic, it must come from God. Equally true, God's people must desire this renewing work of God to happen in their lives. The first priority should be to pray for personal renewal and then for corporate renewal.

One great reward for doing the Lord's work is to witness the renewing work of God in the life of individuals. Nothing can compare with watching people come alive spiritually. And nothing is sadder than watching the institutional church that is supposedly dedicated to God's work stifle individual renewal. When this occurs too often people drift away from the church—as did those leaders whose interviews were cited in Chapter 7. There is a need for the continuing process of organic growth and renewal within the local Body of Christ.

Ideally the assembly will continue as a vibrant and growing organism, always capable of incorporating new growth. Whenever the assembly falls into functioning institutionally rather than as a living organism, its spiritual growth is stifled. At this point it is important that some catalyst begins to work to enhance the renewal process for the assembly to be open to the fresh working of God's Spirit.

The two basic presuppositions upon which this renewal must operate is a general agreement in the fellowship that the church, as the Body of Christ, is to be a worshiping community and witnessing community. Then there must be a felt need for renewal. Until the need for renewal is recognized and localized, the assembly will proceed nowhere. As the questionnaires of the assemblies in North America indicated, the two most common complaints in an assembly are the lack of positive leadership and the lack of vitality. But the two most critical areas to renewal are worship and fellowship. So the local church as the household of God ought to be experiencing renewal in worship and fellowship.

When we pray and work for renewal, we must entertain no illusions for instant results. Charles Swindoll compares renewal to remodeling one's home and says it "will take longer than you planned, cost more than you figured, be messier than you anticipated, and require greater determination than you expected" (1980:10).

Acknowledging this truth, let us consider the components of renewal:

Providing Dynamic Leadership

Although personal renewal can begin at any level, effective corporate renewal of an assembly must involve the leadership. Where it does not, it will only be a matter of time before those personally experiencing renewal either will leave the local assembly or conform to the status quo. As noted this was a main cause for the exodus experienced in the assembles during the last few decades. But what can be done to enhance the possibility of renewal making nonfunctioning elders functional?

A few simple and practical suggestions follow that could go a long way in enhancing leadership renewal.

First of all there must be an openness to change on the part of the elders if renewal is to come. Although change is threatening, if it is done properly, much of the threat can be minimized. For instance, should new leadership be needed the existing elders could agree to individually list potential leaders so that everyone feels some owner-ship of the process. From the collected list of names usually a few names will appear on several lists. These consensus people could then begin a training program approved by the elders, since leaders are made, not born.

Specific leadership training could be utilized in secular seminars on management as well as in religious based training institutions found in most areas of North America. One way is to have the elders attend along with the potential leaders so they could evaluate the program together afterwards. In secular courses, applying these principles to their assembly's needs would be an appropriate tool. This exercise allows the old and new leadership an oppor-tunity to interact with one another and to begin to appreciate and understand one another. Of course it must be remembered that all truth is God's truth, so the principles learned in a secular setting can be beneficial to the local assembly. This approach also takes the pressure off the existing elders who need not feel responsible per-sonally to train the potential leadership.

Of course leadership training with a Christian perspective is easier to apply directly to the local needs of the assembly. In most metropolitan areas evangelical seminaries exist which offer a variety of courses and seminars for lay people on leadership techniques. Again, there is obvious benefit derived from the elders and the leaders-in-process taking these together. The sharing together and the camaraderie developed produce healthy symbols for the rest of the assembly and signal hope that good things are beginning to happen. This could be the beginning of a renewing process.

When hope begins to emerge in the assembly, the younger families will be encouraged to hang in, because change is coming and their needs are going to be met.

This fear of the young and the new on the part of the elders is not only unfortunate, it also contradicts the Brethren's own history. The original Brethren were young people with a vision. As we noted George Muller was 26 and Henry Craik was 27 the year they began working in Bristol. In Dublin when the renewal began, Edward Cronin was 24, John Nelson Darby 27 and John G. Bellett was the old man of the group at 32!

This built-in hesitancy toward allowing the younger set into the eldership, develops an entrenched gerontocracy. What the assemblies need to do is take the time for reflecting on their situation in order to discover creative solutions. Prayerful and thoughtful reflection will always shed light on a situation that might appear irresolvable. However, the entire assembly must be open to evaluation and, where necessary, change. If not, little hope for renewal remains.

Another method to bring about renewal is to challenge the entire congregation to reflect on the qualifications and responsibilities of their leadership. A task force could be directed by an elder or a commended worker who understands the situation and the purpose behind the ministry. Care should be taken that the ministry given is in principle and content what, in fact, the elders feel are their responsibilities. Coming to a consensus on qualification and responsibilities may in itself be the beginning step in the renewing process. The task force may want to go on a weekend retreat or spend some extended time discussing the qualifications and responsibilities of the leadership. Some consensus should be sought, not necessarily unanimous agreement, so that the ministry presented to the whole congregation is manageable. The assembly should be allowed to spend time reflecting on the biblical qualifications for an elder. Care should be taken that the overview is kept in sight. No undue emphasis upon the ideal qualification of an elder need be stressed since no one in the church could match up to the figure which Paul, in both I Timothy 3 and in Titus 1, presents of the ideal elder. These qualifications, taken to their idealistic extreme, would eliminate everyone. What person is completely above reproach in all those areas?

After reflecting on the qualifications of church leaders, other sessions might be dedicated to discussing the responsibilities involved in being an assembly leader. Three areas of responsibility would include: teaching, counseling and ruling. Within these three categories, the congregation can usually recognize those in their midst who meet these responsibilities. At this point they might be asked to formulate a list of possible church elders. Usually it works best when a person is mentioned under a single category. Brief statements could be offered to each suggested name explaining the reasons this person was mentioned. Those who are presently acting as elders could thus be included or omitted on the same basis as everyone else in the assembly.

Such an exercise provides the existing elders with both an evaluation of the current leadership and an understanding of how the congregation feels about potential leaders. Once elders collect this information from the congregation, they must then decide what to do with it. Whatever they do, this information must be handled with wisdom and in confidence. Those elders not supported by the assembly for fulfilling their responsibilities of either teaching, counseling or ruling should seriously consider resigning. It would be best if they would agree before having any congregational discussion that if they do not receive assembly support for their position, they would resign automatically.

This kind of honesty and openness is absolutely essential for renewal. If this procedure for recognition of elders is repeated every three to five years, a more responsive leadership is developed. Of course, in between this procedure, the church leaders should feel free to add and replace elders as they see fit, always being sensitive to the needs and feelings of the assembly as a whole by not appointing someone who does not have their confidence.

This need for a responsive and functioning leadership with spiritual motivation is so great in the assemblies in North America that we cannot allow the methodology of recognizing elders and training future leaders to complicate or prevent us from moving forward or prevent us from doing it. As Walter Liefeld has said:

> It should be apparent that if the biblical ideal of strong, recognized church leadership is not realized, it is small virtue to have avoided error in the relatively less important method of selection. We dare not let our legitimate concern to have a spiritually appropriate method of recognition so paralyze us that we lapse into the un-

certainties of an undefined elderhood or into the grip of a self-proclaimed dictatorship like that of Diotrephes. These perilous alternatives may sometimes arise from failure to realize the importance of the corporate authority of elders (1979:33).

Developing Small Group Fellowships

The local church, to be successful, must function in some degree as the household of God, or practically as family. Ideally, family is a place where one is known and accepted and loved. The same is true in the assembly, yet unfortunately this does not always happen. With a little planning and a lot of prayer, renewal of the local assembly as the household of God can become a reality—especially if one begins to develop small group fellowships as the vehicle for this family atmosphere.

Since there is a tremendous need in our culture for fellowship and since loneliness is the great by-product of our technological society, cultural indicators, like novels, movies and contemporary music, all point to alienation and a need to belong. This need to share and belong is a God-given reality existing in the soul of every human being. In the assembly, this need is met in the whole experience of fellowship. Bruce Larson has made this unusual comparison:

> The neighborhood bar is possibly the best counterfeit there is to the fellowship Christ wants to give to his church. It's an invitation, dispensing liquor instead of grace, escape rather than reality, but it is a permissive, accepting and inclusive fellowship. It is unshockable. It is democratic. You can tell people secrets and they usually don't tell others or even want to. The bar flourishes not because most people are alcoholics, but because God has put into the human heart the desire to know and be known, to love and be loved, and so many seek a counterfeit at the price of a few beers. Christ wants his church to be unshockable, democratic, permissive—a fellowship where people can come in and say "I'm beat!" "I've had it!" (Watson 1979:51).

Christians as well as non-Christians have a great desire to know and be known, to love and be loved. Historically, when the church has experienced renewal, there has been an emphasis on this kind of fellowship. Howard Snyder states:

> Virtually every major movement of spiritual renewal in the Christian church has been accompanied by a return to the small group and the

proliferation of such groups . . . in private homes for Bible study, prayer and the discussion of faith (1982:np).

Donald Bloesch reiterates this analysis throughout his book, *The Evangelical Renaissance* (1973). Certainly the original Brethren renewal demonstrated this, and this need for fellowship is still true today. Interestingly, the rapid growth of the church in South America and in other parts of the Third World can in a large part be attributed to the proliferation of small group fellowships (Cook 1985).

Most small group fellowships in the church have as their purpose the development of a deeper commitment to Jesus Christ. There is a longing to experience what it means to live as a company of committed people in the local assembly. To be the household of God involves a number of specifics. It means to have fellowship with one another— which implies having something in common— sharing in something. Fellowship in the church begins with having a common faith in Jesus Christ and includes sharing that faith with each other. In practicality this means sharing what God is doing in our lives, encouraging one another in the faith (Heb 3:13; 10: 24-25), and praying for one another within a loving group. It also implies studying the Word of God together in an atmosphere of openness and honesty, caring for one another and meeting people at their points of weakness— not always at their points of strength. In essence, it means being Jesus Christ with one another in Christ.

Among the many people who have commented on the value of small group fellowship, Kevin Thompson has pointed out that they can be:

1. Flexible. Small groups can be adapted to any group. They are able to change structure and direction easily. They can meet on different nights in diverse situations.

2. Mobile. Small groups are not tied to one fixed location. They can meet where convenient.

3. [Laity]-led. Small groups require a minimum of professional leadership. They avoid a focus on a specially trained clergy. Small groups allow for the full exercise of the priesthood of all believers.

4. Inclusive. Small groups can involve everyone in the Body. They are small enough so that each person is provided personal attention. No one needs to be ignored or overlooked in ministry.

5. Natural. Small groups bring Christianity back into the home, the cell unit out of which the church is made. The love and life of

Christ brought right into the home will do much to restore relationships and order in the home.

6. Personal. In small groups sharing of lives takes place in intimate settings. Many people who don't feel close or committed to others in large group meetings can establish close contacts in small groups.

7. Evangelistic. Small groups are an extension of the church in the secular society. They provide an effective means of low-keyed, friendship evangelism. Many non-Christians will go to a house meeting who wouldn't go near a church building. In small groups, people are receptive to the gospel message.

8. Reproductive. Small groups can grow, divide and multiply naturally yet stay small and personal.

9. Productive. Small groups provide workable sizes for identifying and developing specific gifts, ministries and services. Each group can be made accountable for active ministry involvement. There is a ministry to be found for everyone in small groups (1982:18).

Some further specific suggestions for developing small group fellowships in the local assembly follow, although it must be pointed out that without the Holy Spirit's involvement, no strategy will be successful, so the whole plan must be a matter of constant dependence upon God as evidenced in prayer.

To begin, a small group fellowship committee could be formed consisting of at least three people. It will insure an easier acceptance into the group if one of these is an elder who shares the vision of what a small group ministry could become. This person could then act as a liaison with the other elders.

A second person, selected from the congregation at large, could hold what will be a most important role— that of the small group coordinator. This should be a person fully convinced of the ministry of small groups and enthusiastically willing to invest time and energy into making it work. As the future resident expert on the dynamics of small group fellowships, this person needs the endorsement and support of the elders, because without their support, the fellowship groups have little hope of succeeding. Beyond being committed to growth through small groups, the elders must also be willing to budget the necessary funds to help make it work.

The other member of this trio could act as a small group fellowship consultant and if necessary, this person could be drawn in from outside the assembly. What this person would ideally provide this committee is some expertise or training in developing small groups in the local church. Such facilitators are relatively easy to find. Every evangelical seminary has interns being trained in either Christian education or church growth who have special talents in developing small groups. Often these students are required to have practical experience in a local church before they can graduate, so such a pool which can help establish small groups are often only a phone call away. Beyond this, professional church consulting agencies exist who have trained specialists eager to help the local churches develop an effective small groups operation. As an expert in the field of small groups, the consultant's primary purpose is to help train the small group coordinator or direct the first stages of the small group process.

After the small group committee is formed, trained and ready to move into action they can proceed with the preparation of a written statement which sets forth the general biblical and theological goals for building and developing Christian community in the assembly. A professional consultant is usually helpful at this point because they are normally current on the literature available on small groups. Such a written statement might also set forth the goals for the number and types of small groups projected for the assembly in a three- to five-year time frame. A healthy goal might be establishing 20 small groups over a five-year period, with 75% of the congregation involved. It cannot be stated too emphatically though: Goals are an absolute necessity. If you don't know where you are going, you won't get there.

One effective method that the small group committee could employ is a careful evaluation of the congregation to determine where the networks of Christian community actually are functioning. What small groups already are meeting during the week? Are there groups that meet periodically for social reasons? What small groups go out to dinner after the Sunday service? It is vital to take advantage of these natural fellowships because small groups, to be effective, must not try to take the place of any groups currently in existence. Rather, the committee should seek ways to strengthen these existing networks of small groups in order to produce a successful program.

Various subgroups within the congregation could be targeted in order to evaluate the likelihood of their responsiveness and openness to small groups. Usually a tremendous potential for small groups exists among the young marrieds or those new to the assembly.

Other potential fellowships might be a support group for working women or for single parents. The existing needs of a particular assembly will, of course, determine what groups are tried. At this point the questionnaire helps target the needy areas and sub-groups within the assembly.

Ideally, the small group committee should develop a prototype small group, carefully selecting them from the key subgroups in the assembly so as to get a good cross section of the congregation. Hopefully these will eventually become the small group leaders of the second generation groups that will form after having had a successful experience in the prototype group. By carefully recruiting a group of up to twelve people, this base or model group should include the future coordinator of the small groups and the representative elders, as well as representatives of the most needy sub-groups in the congregation.

At this juncture it is well to turn to the guidance of the consultant who can help organize the small group experience. Some suggested steps would include:

1). The model group should write their own contract or covenant which is a shared understanding by *all* the participants as regards their purpose and the general means that will be used to achieve that purpose. At this point many groups fail. Unless there is a mutual ownership of purpose, there will never be commitment to any of the three areas normally involved: studying, praying and sharing together.

2). Some agreement on commitment needs to be made. This could be "To Christ, to one another, to the purpose of the group through the agreed disciplines of regular attendance, participation, study, prayer for each other and confidentiality." The normal length of commitment for the group is between eight and twelve weeks. It is important to have a definite closure time. Should a group decide to continue longer once this period is up, it is important to close and recontract and start a new cycle. Regular attendance is also important and everyone should be serious about expecting to give a weekly commitment of a couple hours from each person.

3). The model group should be committed to caring for one another. This, practically, means that there would be open and healthy sharing of personal needs. It also follows that the group would do all they could to meet those needs, whether they are physical, spiritual, financial or emotional. This, of course, would be done in an atmosphere of strict confidentiality.

4). The model group should also be committed to growth through study of the scriptures and subjects pertinent to the Christian faith. Jesus Christ must remain the center of this fellowship for without the centrality of Christ, genuine growth will not take place. Finally, the actual process of study and prayer should be done in an atmosphere of warm acceptance without pressure.

Throughout this period the small group committee should continue to develop a strategy for seeking to improve the quality of the Christian community in the existing small groups. This might mean working with the existing small groups and the already-existing fellowships, not stifling them by giving the attention to the model group or allowing an elitist attitude to develop that could create a backlash toward an existing group.

As the model group progresses through their agreed upon cycle, the consultant or the coordinator should gradually turn the leadership over to the group. Throughout the whole time the consultant should be acting as a coach to the coordinator and the group participants, acting only as a resource person for the group— supplying helpful books, materials and insights necessary for leading a group.

Then as the model nears the end of their experience, the small group committee should begin to publicize the process in order to inform and impress on the whole congregation the importance and value of such small groups. This could be done through the preaching ministry, through personal testimonies of those in the model group or through personal contacts. Of course, if the model group has not been a success, there is no selling the program to the whole congregation.

But ideally the project is working, so stage two of the small group experience consists of formulating four to six new groups, each with a leadership team that had been part of the original model group. Each of these experienced small group participants can thus return to a particular subgroup and help that small group fellowship follow the same pattern they were taught in the model group. Of course the content of the contract would not remain the same—that would be determined by the group contract, but the basic process would be patterned on the model in order to develop a shared understanding by all in the group of the purpose and means that will be used to achieve their goal.

The small group committee can now be used as a resource team to the congregation as a whole and with the leaders of the small groups recruit and train potential leaders that surface with the second generation groups. Usually this means that the small group coordinator will have to give a lot of individual attention to potential leaders that surface, and some special training sessions may be in order at this point.

A suggested timetable for developing small groups might be: September— forming a small group committee; October— recruiting prototype small groups; October 15 through Christmas— the model group in process; January through Easter— the formulation of four to six new small groups; after Easter until June 20— the recontracting and beginning of new groups; summer break and a time to evaluate and prepare for the next year. Such a timetable should be flexible to meet emergencies and other needs of the group.

If such a strategy succeeds, there will be a proliferation of small groups— all of which could help the local assembly in its process of experiencing renewal through small group fellowship.

Enhancing Renewal Through Worship

The research cited earlier pointed out that the lack of vitality in worship is one basic reason there is a decline among the assemblies. Specific studies conducted by Lois Fleming have shown that attendance there is poor in comparison with the Family Bible Hour. Related to this is the surprising statistic that indicates the majority of assemblies see the need for it and would welcome change and new growth (1984:24-24). This does not indicate that the average congregation is ready for a full-fledged revision of its worship service, only that there is a healthy atmosphere that would welcome some change. Where the leadership is not aware of this trend or is insensitive to this mood in the congregation, it will only create more dissatisfaction. At this point a large portion of the congregation may begin to drop out of the worship service. This is what we would like to preclude.

Worship has always been a vital part of the life in the church. Richard Lovelace states:

> In the history of movements of spiritual renewal . . . it is apparent that where the truths embodied in the Lord's supper are clearly taught and proclaimed, spiritual renewal is present, but where the sacraments are administered without much explanation, simply as a kind of spiritual medicine, a palpable deadness may set in (1980:170).

Today a renaissance of worship is occurring in many evangelical churches. This is relatively easy to document by reading the major Christian periodicals which regularly describe current worship phenomena such as the Calvary Chapel movement. This is not to say that such renewal movements are free of problems, but there is no denying that renewal and growth are taking place and interestingly, usually key to these renewal movements is worship. Over and over these tend to stress the importance of collective worship which brings us to a difficult question: If worship is the key to renewal, why are the Brethren congregations not experiencing renewal, since worship is the central part of our tradition? A deeply troubling question like this can have no pat answers. Surely, part of the answer is locked into our history and the negative influence that exclusivism has had on worship. I would posit that J.N. Darby long ago distorted the concept of worship so thoroughly that the effects are still evident even today. It is these negative effects which must be addressed if ever we are to overcome the current malaise. We must begin to emphasize a positive strategy of worship.

The following is a sample practical suggestion:

A Need for More Praise and Spontaneity

One of the puzzling aspects of the Lord's Supper is that in format there appears to be a great deal of room for spontaneity, yet practically very little is ever experienced.

Our research questionnaire specifically queried the respondent regarding their experience of expectancy at the Lord's Supper. Amazingly, of this group the majority participating in the worship services do not experience a sense of expectancy or excitement. With all the space made available for spontaneity and the leading of the Holy Spirit, one should hope for more of a sense of anticipation. When this does not happen in the worship service of the average assembly, one can only assume that there are inhibiting factors working in counterproductive ways.

When very few new or fresh voices are heard in the worship service or when many simply stay away, the easy assumption to make is that this indicates some spiritual problem. Lack of attendance at the Lord's Supper is interpreted as lack of love for the Lord or lack of interest in true worship. While in some cases this may be true, it is a rather serious charge to level against a believer and it is a charge which, in many cases, is refuted by active participation in other areas of assembly life. It would seem that it is more likely that fear, based on unfamiliarity with the unwritten "rules" for appropriate participation, plus a perceived resistance to ways of expressing worship, are the main factors which inhibit spontaneity and cause many to choose not to attend the worship service. Should this be true, then it will take more than exhortations from the pulpit and in the bulletin to get people to choose to attend.

While it is biblically correct to say that a believer ought to attend the Lord's Supper, it is also important that a believer be able to enjoy worship as well. God desires joyful worship. That the worship service is intended to be a time of giving to God ought not be used as an excuse for ignoring the fact that many are, quite frankly, not enthused by what they see at the worship service. They still love Jesus Christ. They are not bored with worship. They are simply not moved to worship by what they perceive to be the only "acceptable" ways to express worship at the Lord's Supper.

Basically, no changes in format of the worship service are required. Spontaneity and freedom are already allowed for in a way that many advocates of renewal in other traditions long for. The problem appears to be what many perceive, rightly or wrongly, to be very strict limits on that freedom and spontaneity. A feeling pervades that any contribution has to be "just so" or a person will be judged out of line. Compounding the problem is the fact that those limits are never clearly spelled out or discussed but are left implicit. This leaves many people vulnerable as to what is acceptable, especially young Christians and those whose backgrounds are not in the assemblies. The solution for this is not a major change in the format of the Lord's Supper but rather in the way it is perceived.

But the question is raised whether or not the fears and perceived strictures on freedom are real or not. Undoubtedly, the fear on the part of some teenagers that the older Christians do not want them to say anything until they can do it eloquently is largely unfounded. This natural fear is a part of growing up. On the other hand, when 30-year-old adults with children in the Sunday school choose not to attend a meeting because they feel that the ways they like to express worship or the songs they like would not be accepted, we are not dealing with a manufactured fear. Somehow, they have received messages, either intended or incidental, that only certain forms of worship are acceptable. This problem is serious, and no change in time, place or format will resolve it.

Those perceived as insiders need to ask themselves whether they are willing to accept and appreciate the way other believers express their worship, even if it is not in accordance with their own style. If such acceptance is not given, it would seem there is a serious problem of spiritual pride and lack of love to be dealt with before renewal will ever come.

Where different styles are tolerated, the entrenched church members should then ask themselves whether they are communicating in subtle ways an unwillingness to accept another person's way of expressing worship. The answer to this question is most effectively answered by those who do not attend the service. Asking such a person whether there is anything about one's attitude which makes them uncomfortable in sharing at the Lord's Supper might not be an easy question, but when a nonattender is able to answer this honestly, new insights into the makeup of the church can be learned.

The elders must take the lead in this process and be the first to ask themselves these questions. They must also encourage others to follow their lead. To continue to ask publicly, "What is wrong with the spiritual lives of those who do not attend the Lord's Supper?" cannot possibly result in anything other than effecting an obligatory attendance at the Lord's Supper—and it probably will not even accomplish that.

Christ wants people to attend his banquet because they desire to come and enjoy worshiping him—not because they feel they are obligated to come. There are plenty of angels and other creatures who will worship at his command. Of those he made in his image, he desires a free and joyous worship. Until these perceived fears and inhibitions discussed above are dealt with, it is unlikely that the attendance and participation levels at the worship service will increase.

Music is a particularly powerful way of both stimulating and expressing worship. Note the close relationship between singing and being filled with the Spirit: "Be filled with the Spirit. Speak to one another with psalms, hymns and spiritual songs. Sing and make music in your heart to the Lord" (Ep 5:18-19). Singing is the expression of the emotions of the soul. If music reflects the language of the soul, then our Christian music ought to reflect our relationship to God. James says, "Is anyone happy? Let him sing songs of praise" (5:13). Paul says, "Let the word of Christ dwell in you richly as you teach and admonish one another with all wisdom, and as you *sing* psalms, hymns and spiritual songs with gratitude in your hearts to God" (Col 3:16).

God loves music. He especially loves new music because it is a reflection of one's growing relationship with him. The adjective "new" is used more frequently in scriptures with the noun "song" than any other word (Young 1955:694). The biblical mandate often follows the following passage:

Sing joyfully to the Lord, you righteous; it is fitting for the upright to praise him. Praise the Lord with the harp; make music to him on the ten-stringed lyre. Sing a *new* song; play skillfully, and shout for joy (Ps 33:1-3).

Or again: "He lifted me out of the pit. . . He put a new song in my mouth, a hymn of praise to our God" (Ps 40:2-3). "Sing to the Lord a *new* song, sing to the Lord, all the earth. Sing to the Lord, praise his name" (Ps 96:1-2). "Sing to the Lord a *new* song, for he has done marvelous things" (Ps 98:1). "I will sing a *new* song to you, O God; on the ten-stringed lyre I will make music to you" (Ps 144:9). "Praise the Lord. Sing to the Lord a new song, his praise in the assembly of the saints" (Ps 149:1).

God not only loves new music, he loves loud music. We read that "David and all the Israelites were celebrating with all their might before God, with songs and with harps, lyres, tambourines, cymbals and trumpets" (1 Ch 13:8). It is interesting to note what scriptures say about the trained choirs and musicians whose primary purpose in life was to sing and play instruments to the glory of God as is told us in Exodus (15:20-21), 1 Samuel (10:5) or 1 Chronicles (16:4-5, 23:5).

Obviously God loves music because it reflects a heart filled with love and praise. Not only in ancient Israel did God love music, he loves music in the Christian church. Jesus in the upper room led the disciples in singing a hymn before they left the upper room (Mt 26:30). When Paul and Silas were imprisoned in Philippi, in the middle of the night they were singing hymns to God (Ac 16:25). In the Corinthian church the believers were encouraged to bring hymns to the meeting (1 Co 14:26). Scholars feel the New Testament is filled with fragments of what were the hymns and doxologies that the Christians sang in the church—the most famous being the christological hymn in Philippians (2:5-11). Recent evidence even shows that this hymn was originally composed in Aramaic and sung at the celebration of the Lord's Supper by the church in Palestine (Martin 1965:106). This evidence, connected with the passages where music is linked to joy and spiritual fulness (Ep 5:18-19; Co 3:16; Jm 5:13), conclusively prove that God loves music because it is a reflection of the soul language of his people.

Since music is an emotional indicator of one's spiritual growth, it becomes obvious why God wants new songs to be sung to him. He wants evidence that his people are growing in their relationship to him. This is not to imply that the great hymns of the faith are to be discarded for contemporary Christian music. It simply means there must be an avenue for praise and spontaneity in worship. New music is an obvious way to introduce more joy and celebration into our collective worship.

D. L. Moody concurred when he said in 1879, "If you want to wake up fresh interest in your churches, have some new music" (Dinwiddie 1982). One of the contemporary songs Moody advocated was "Crown Him With Many Crowns" (Dinwiddie 1982). Bryan J. Leech, a contemporary music writer, made this penetrating observation concerning music in the church:

> To me, the ideal church, musically speaking, is one in which music is drawn from all traditions and all eras, where the mix is eclectic and varied, catering to a wide variety of tastes. So that in any given service of worship there is something to satisfy the devout classicist and something to please the one with nothing more than a liking for a good tune. Not only does such an approach give a richness to the music program but it also teaches us a very important practical lesson, a lesson about love.

> In his eloquent letter to the Corinthian church, St. Paul defines love as that quality "which suffers long and is kind" which "does not boast and is not proud." So often we expect our churches to reflect our likes and dislikes and we're extremely vocal if things don't go our way. Yet so often the things we insist upon, important as they may seem to be, are really peripheral matters, for what is really vital is that we learn to love and respect and support people with tastes quite different from our own. For the only thing that needs to be held in common for a genuine church to exist is Jesus Christ and the truth of his death and resurrection. Anything else held in common is really a bonus, an extra, a nonessential but nice addition (1982:17).

It appears to be clear that God loves music and that music can be a way to encourage more spontaneity and joy in the Lord's Supper. The following are some specific suggestions that might be helpful in creating more praise and spontaneity and hopefully enhance renewal in our hearts.

Specific Suggestions

1. The leadership could begin to increase their awareness of church renewal by selectively reading the literature that is available. This could include books such as *Furnace of Renewal* (a vision for the church) by George Mallone. This book is of particular interest since Mallone comes from the Brethren tradition. *The Problem*

of Wineskins and *The Community of the King,* both written by Howard Snyder, are also excellent resource books. Larry Richards and Clyde Hoeldtke have written a valuable book called *A Theology of Church Leadership.* Other good book titles are listed in the bibliography.

Book discussions might be scheduled so that by a particular date one agreed-upon book will have been read by all the elders of the assembly. One elder can lead a discussion regarding it or give an oral book report or even pass out a written reaction paper to be shared with the group. This could happen at a regularly scheduled elders' meeting or at a retreat. Along with such literature study, other profitable themes could be examined such as a study of worship from the scriptures. Aids for such biblical study should be provided so that the elders could read the articles on worship from reference works such as: *The New International Dictionary of New Testament Theology, The Interpreter's Dictionary of the Bible,* or the *Theological Dictionary of the New Testament.*

2. The elders could also take advantage of the available courses offered at local evangelical seminaries (located in almost every major metropolitan area) on church renewal and church growth. These courses are not limited to full-time seminary students. Although such action may be impractical and economically unfeasible for all elders, still it would be beneficial if the local assembly could sponsor one or two elders to attend. They in turn could make a written or oral report to the rest of the elders, sharing with them some of the suggestions they have learned in order to implement what they had learned on the assembly-wide scale.

3. The leadership could sponsor one of their own to visit and get thoroughly acquainted with what is happening in an assembly that is experiencing growth in numbers and renewal in worship. A few of the assemblies in North America that are currently experiencing either growth or renewal in worship include the *University Chapel* in Vancouver, British Columbia, the *Hayward Bible Chapel* in Hayward, California, the *Fairhaven Bible Chapel* in San Leandro, California, the *Laurel Park Bible Chapel* Portland, Oregon, the *Believer's Chapel* in Dallas, Texas, and the *Dunning Park Bible Chapel* in Detroit, Michigan. Others also exist. By getting in touch with one of these assemblies and arranging for one or more elders to visit and observe what is happening, they will be able to meet and experience the atmosphere of growth and renewal in such an assembly. Hopefully such encounters will prove contagious.

4. After having personal exposure and experience with an assembly in the process of either renewal or growth, the leadership could begin to implement some renewal ideas into their own assembly by forming a worship committee composed of representatives from the major subgroups in the assembly. Praise and renewal music could also be gradually introduced to the congregation. Praise albums could be played in the fellowship areas of the chapel at appropriate times, like at the coffee breaks, which would acquaint the congregation with new music. Praise music and renewal songs could also be planned in the music portion of the Family Bible Hour. Hymns could be selected with more variety and continuity with the sermon or an overhead projector could be used to introduce the newer renewal music.

Perhaps a monthly Lord's Supper could be planned in the regular Family Bible Hour. Although it would be in an abbreviated form, this would serve to introduce the Lord's Supper to those who never come or are unfamiliar with an open participatory-type communion service. This has been practiced by a number of assemblies with great success.

Another method would be to periodically schedule praise concerts on a Sunday evening. These concerts could be planned in a way so that the whole congregation would feel comfortable attending. For instance there are a lot of worship albums that are simply the psalms put to music. It would be great to have an evening with the whole congregation learning these new worship songs. It might be preferable to have ministry at the Family Bible Hour or just prior to the concert on the importance of joy and praise in the Christian life. Actually, a series of messages on the importance of joy and celebration in the Christian's life would always be helpful.

Another renewal project might be to have the worship committee plan, in a minimal way, the direction of the Lord's Supper. For instance, worship themes could be prearranged the week before with suggested passages to be meditated upon throughout the week. There would be the planned introduction of a new song through the use of an overhead projector. A person could be chosen to introduce the theme and begin the worship service. The worship committee could also plan an occasional creative worship service on Sunday evening which would be a time when people are encouraged to bring their musical instruments and songs that they have written or poetry they would like to share—all aimed at worshiping God. This meeting would need to be orchestrated carefully, yet it could be a tremendous celebration of worship.

These suggestions are in no way profound or radical in nature, but all of them would enhance renewal in any assembly that wants to experience the freshness of God's Spirit. Worship is central to renewal. The Lord's Supper is the center of worship— not the circumference of worship. Of course worship is much broader than the communion service—encompassing a life-style, service to God as well as one's personal daily experience. The scripture speaks a lot about these broader concepts of worship which must be the subject of a further study than what is incorporated here.

George Mallone cites a description of a vision of worship which he found in a Sunday bulletin of a church that was experiencing renewal. This would be my prayer for all the assemblies that genuinely want to experience the life of God in their midst.

> *We believe* worship of God should be spiritual. *Therefore:* We remain flexible and yielded to the leading of the Spirit to direct our worship. *We believe* worship of God should be inspirational. *Therefore:* We give a great place to music in our worship. *We believe* worship of God should be intelligent. *Therefore:* Our services are designed with great emphasis upon teaching the Word God that he might instruct how he should be worshiped. *We believe* worship of God should be sacramental. *Therefore:* we give ourselves to weekly observance of the Lord's Supper. *We believe* worship of God is fruitful. *Therefore:* We look for his love in our lives as the supreme manifestation that we have truly been worshiping him (1981:76-77).

In Conclusion

14

Proverbs tells us, "Where there is no vision, the people perish" (29:18). This insight particularly is relevant to congregations that come from the Plymouth Brethren tradition. No one likes to face cold, unpleasant facts. But there is no escaping it—the Plymouth Brethren in the United States are in decline.

Though the reasons for this decline are complex, still our interviews with a large number of former as well as current Brethren leaders and elders, indicated that the overriding cause of dissatisfaction is seen in the leadership. Because the Plymouth Brethren tradition is based upon the priesthood of all believers, it functionally becomes a lay movement, with great responsibility placed in the hands of the elders. Often the church elders have failed to realize the importance of their own leadership position or to train the younger generation to take their place. Consequently a leadership crisis exists throughout the Brethren assemblies, and without a vision at the top, erosion at the bottom becomes inevitable.

This erosion process attacks every aspect of the assembly. Where there is no vision, the congregation lacks a sense of direction. The local assembly is not going anywhere because there are no tangible goals or concrete plans to achieve anything. Aiming at nothing, the assemblies find themselves successfully creating an atmosphere of discouragement.

With no vision or positive leadership, the local assembly becomes distorted, the pulpit ministry thrives on mediocrity, and worship—always the key distinctive of the Brethren—becomes predictable and lifeless. Minor doctrinal differences explode and divide assembly from assembly and the Brethren, as a whole, from the broader evangelical church.

Unfortunately many Brethren seem unaware of the dynamics causing their own demise. In many instances a built-in parochialism acts as a defense mechanism preventing them from accepting criticism. An attitude of uninformed arrogance regrettably runs throughout the Brethren.

The need for renewal is obvious among the Brethren. Renewal, in order to be authentic, must be fundamentally grounded in the Word of God. The New Testament has a lot to say about the church. One of the most amazing things the New Testament says about the church is that both the universal church and the local church have a part in God's cosmic plan for the universe. God is accomplishing his purposes through the church. One's concept of the church, thus, is of primary importance because it will determine how one relates to other Christians and to the world.

The New Testament simply does not present the church in a technical or doctrinal way for it is not to be read as a textbook on ecclesiology. Rather, the New Testament presents the church as a live and living organism and uses many different images and metaphors to describe the relationship between the church and Christ. Each metaphor presents a different angle of truth concerning the living relationship that Christ has with the church.

The four metaphors chosen here stress varying aspects. The church as a temple of God underlies the importance of its stance as a worshiping community. The church as the household of God describes the local church as family, with all that implies. The church called to be the people of God is the witnessing church. The church as the Body of Christ helps us understand church structure. After all, the church is not to be understood as solely an institution; it must be seen in all its mystery as a living organism. In some ways, the church involves a mystical extension of the life of Christ on earth today. We must insist on maintaining the mystical element of the church, and we must resist those who would interpret and reduce the body of Christ to an institution only.

The original Brethren from Ireland and England, who were all part of the institutional church, began to seek renewal as they began to experience the church as a living and growing reality. Historically, they were a small part of a long line of reformational and renewal movements. The principles John Wyclif advocated some 500 years earlier were intuitively and spontaneously rediscovered. The Puritans, the Quakers and the Wesleyans made significant contributions to the renewal movement of the 1830s and 1840s.

The immediate cause of the renewal movement was dissatisfaction with the established church (the Anglican church) and the dissenting churches (the independent churches). The former was perceived as a corrupt institution while the latter were considered separatistic and sectarian. The middle ground was what the Brethren sought. The established church had unity without purity and the dissenting churches claimed purity without any unity.

The mood was set for reform and unity. Through the influence of Anthony Norris Groves, an Anglican layperson, a surprising number of young Anglican students studying for the priesthood began to seek reform and renewal in the church. Their motive was to meet in the name of the Lord Jesus only. The Lord's Supper became the sacrament of unity. All who claimed the name of the Lord Jesus were welcome. Spontaneously, small groups began to meet throughout England, and Oxford, Plymouth and Bristol became centers for renewal. Dublin became the focal point of reform and renewal in Ireland.

Ironically, these groups were brought together by the study of prophecy, although no consensus was reached among the early Brethren on the finer points of interpreting prophecy. They all, however, agreed the condition of the church was deplorable and that reform and unity must be sought.

In seeking reform and unity, this little band intuitively began to model themselves on the biblical images of the church— allowing the church to be the church, the household of God to one another and the temple of God in corporate worship. They did this all in the context of a living relationship in the Body of Christ, functioning organically as the Body of Christ. This renewal produced phenomenal growth and all of England, Ireland and Scotland felt its effects.

But to have a united church and pure church proved to be an elusive synthesis. Without a creed, the Brethren were subject to the influence of their leaders— many well-qualified, but none equal to John Nelson Darby in popularity. Unfortunately, Darby's obsession with prophecy eventually caused him to develop a theological system of thought which actually undermined the very renewal that he had played such an integral part in initiating. Finally Darby's doctrine of the church in ruin distorted every rediscovered truth the early Brethren had found so that what truth remains is distorted in its application.

Darby's influence is far broader than most realize. The unwritten assumptions which sprang from his brand of exclusivism are very much a part of those who claim to be of the open wing of the Brethren, even though a large percentage of those have never heard of John Nelson Darby. The unwritten rules that govern their worship meeting as well as the parochialism and the lack of recognized offices in the church all come from Darby's distortions.

So we are left with the question of how the Brethren can regain their original vision which was based solidly on a biblical perspective. Fresh understanding of the purpose of the church is needed if the local church is to be an organism and not merely an institution.

Also the assemblies must distinguish between principles and practices. Assemblies historically have failed at this point, assuming the traditions of the Brethren, with all the distortions, without distinguishing the difference between biblical principle and contemporary practice. To assume, as the Brethren often do, that our method of worship is the biblical model is to confuse the principle of worship with mode of worship. Emphasis falls on worshiping correctly rather than simply on worshiping. Form and procedure take precedence over praise and thanksgiving.

Closely associated with the inability to distinguish between principle and practice is the attitude that right doctrine is the basis of fellowship and acceptance. The church is not seen organically as a family of believers but rather as a repository of right beliefs. When this kind of atmosphere exists, social forces begin to create a unity-through-conformity mentality which becomes extremely counter-productive to the church as the Body of Christ. On the other hand, when the assembly functions organically, relational values are stressed and members are bound together by loyalty.

Finally, we come to the task of actually implementing a strategy that might enhance renewal. Again, it should be stated that renewal is a work of God. Apart from the Spirit of God working in the people of God, all our strategies will amount to nothing. Also, renewal cannot be forced upon those who are not interested. There are those of the Plymouth Brethren tradition who are totally satisfied with their current condition. But to those who desire renewal, there must be an acceptance of their impoverished condition and a willingness to change.

The first step is to have an open and honest evaluation of the local assembly (see sample questionnaire in the Appendix B). Every area of the assembly should be evaluated—leadership, midweek meetings and the worship service. Such a questionnaire, which can be analyzed with a computer, can tell a great deal about the dynamics of an assembly.

Then based on this evaluation, the second step is to develop some specific strategies to enhance renewal. This could be a leadership training program for the younger generation, or it could be developing a specific plan to inform the congregation of the qualifications and responsibilities of the elders so they can recognize those who are qualified and doing the work of an elder. This might be threatening to some, but it is essential if the tide of poor leadership is ever going to be changed.

Establishing a small group program will allow the assembly to experience what it means to become the household of God and be brought to a deeper commitment to Jesus Christ. The mutual sharing of joys and sorrows will enrich the spiritual life of the congregation.

Finally, the key to lasting corporate renewal is worship. Where renewal is transforming churches, worship becomes central. Renewal brings worship. Worship brings renewal. That is the nature of the Body of Christ and the purpose of the church being the temple of God. One cannot form a strategy for the Holy Spirit. One can only prepare new wineskins in hopes of his filling. Ironically, the assemblies already provide space for this, but there are few assemblies experiencing the joy of renewal and spontaneous worship.

It is true that renewal can produce renewal, but first, one must share the vision of renewal—either through the literature of renewal or through visiting renewed and growing assemblies and churches. Practical steps could be taken to introduce praise music into both the worship and ministry meetings or by asking a worship committee to give more guidance to the breaking of bread.

Renewal will only come when God's people truly desire it and when God freely gives it. We all are to be part of this renewing of our minds which was in Christ Jesus.

Appendix A
Interviews, Topically Grouped

Lack of Positive Leadership

A former Brethren who was president of a Christian liberal arts college declared:

> There is a structural flaw in the Brethren. They do not train people for ministry in a serious way. . . . Consequently, elders are serving virtually as popes. The problems are they are ignorant and arrogant and they are powerful.

A full-time worker (for 35 years) who is also an elder said:

> A big problem is seen in the attitude "once an elder, always an elder." There is no thought of reproducing yourself or training younger men to step into positions of responsibility.

A further problem for the serious and committed elder was well stated by an elder from the Midwest who said:

> The number one difficulty with our eldership is a practical one. Each elder has more than a full-time job outside the church. All the elders have responsible positions in their professions. If you think of elders as shepherds, they are really not doing the job. We should be spending a large portion of our time taking care of the sheep. That is just not happening.

A noted full-time worker from the Midwest, who is one of the leading voices in the Brethren movement, said:

> The problem in all the assemblies is that they lack a staff. There is no full-time staff and, therefore, there is no accountability. It is a defect in the system. The assemblies will not be renewed until there are structural changes. These changes must provide for leadership.

Another full-time worker and writer who is a seminary graduate, made an important observation:

> There are assemblies looking for full-time workers and there are seminary graduates who are available, but there is no mechanism to join the two. We tried to develop a mechanism to bring the need and supply together but not with any success.

When pushed further on why the two could not be brought together, this person said:

> Seminaries are geared to train professionals the same way a medical school or law school trains professionals. The assembly system is not geared for professionals.

One of the most respected commended workers in North America made a startling comment with regard to the leadership crisis in the assemblies:

> If I were starting over, I would either be in a para-church ministry or I would be a pastor. I would not settle into the assemblies as a place for a life of ministry. The reason I would not settle in the assemblies is there isn't adequate scope for the ministry that is needed. The kind of work that is required in the assembly demands a full-time teacher and preacher ministry. I know of no assembly, with the possible exception of one, that would permit that. There just isn't any scope for this kind of ministry in our denomination. I would go elsewhere.

Lack of Vitality

One very energetic person who is now an elder in a large church made this point:

> We made repeated efforts to stem the tide of a declining situation, but we were utterly stifled by the leadership. When attendance at the midweek Bible study at the chapel dropped, we tried to convince the elders of midweek home Bible studies. They refused. When it became obvious to most that the elders were getting old and ineffective, the deacons tried to institute some form of training for future elders. The elders stifled that. We tried to get the best gifted men on the platform, those who spoke to real needs. The elders stifled that also. My repeated attempts to do something about our dying condition only got me labeled as a troublemaker.

One man, formerly from a Seattle assembly, gave this story of frustration and burnout:

> I was the Sunday school superintendent. I was responsible for K through junior high and I taught the class for junior high through college age. I could not get any help. I would cry out for help and the people were not interested. I felt absolutely drained. I went to the elders about the class I was teaching and they agreed it should be divided up, but they were not willing to help. No one ever gave me any direction or evaluated what was being done. As long as you

were busy and regularly attended the meetings, that's all that mattered, especially the Breaking of Bread meeting. But we were crying on the inside because nobody even asked us how we were doing spiritually. Now (in the Baptist church) I'm involved in a one-on-one ministry and we meet regularly for sharing and praying.

This man was going through some particularly hard times in his marriage and family and no one in the assembly offered to help, which only intensified the problem of discouragement in the assembly.

Declining assemblies tend to take hard-line positions regarding relational problems. One active member of an East coast assembly attested to this:

> On the East coast there are a lot more dwindling, little assemblies than there are growing, larger assemblies... Those assemblies that are growing are sensitive to the needs of their young people and are future-looking... Also, the assemblies that are growing have somehow been able to accept people who have failed— those with marital problems, those with children problems— whereas the dwindling assemblies somehow succeed in not accepting these people or in some way ostracizing them.

Dissatisfaction with the Pulpit Ministry

Discouragement over the quality of pulpit ministry is seen in the comments of a former youth worker from Cleveland:

> My needs were not being met, especially in the area of Bible teaching. There was not any consistent Bible teaching. There was no unified plan for ministry. The problem was the philosophy of ministry. Sunday morning, 11 AM Family Bible Hour, was always evangelistic. . . . The quality of ministry in comparison to the church I'm going to now was poor. This was due mainly to the circuit-riding preachers that made continuity impossible.

The following are technical and practical comments that came from a number of highly-educated people about the quality of the pulpit ministry:

> It troubled me so much that many leading Brethren did their sermon preparation by the case of first impression. They used only their Bibles, prayer and the *Reader's Digest*. There was a complete rejection of scholars and commentaries.

Another third generation ex-Brethren, who holds a Ph.D. and teaches in a Christian liberal arts college, carried this observation further:

> Brethren come to the scriptures with a grid system that they impose on the scriptures rather than allowing the Word to speak freely. They place great restraint on the Spirit when it comes to interpreting the scriptures. The Brethren have a confined idea of how the Holy Spirit works. The picture one gets is that you are to sit at home with your Bible on your lap and expect the Holy Spirit to equip and teach you.

Another elder who is active in an assembly in the Northwest and who holds a Ph.D. in history essentially agreed that the grid system imposed upon the Bible is "mindless dispensationalism which kills vitality and growth" and that to hold the doctrine of the priesthood of all believers to an extreme position would ultimately water down the gifts of the Spirit and produce mediocrity of ministry.

One elder and full-time worker, 60 years of age and still in school seeking more education, said, "Many times whoever is on the platform bores me to the point of frustration."

A successful ex-Brethren attorney stated:

> From the beginning the lay preaching type of thing was a terrible millstone around my neck because the assemblies have always expected everyone to leap off their seats and talk. . . . I have never been much of a fan of this lay preacher kind of thing. I'd far rather listen to someone who knows what they are is talking about . . . For years and years I have been very aware that the Brethren taught a party line. There was never any room for any questioning or divergency of thought. Anyone who did question or had a different viewpoint was made to feel very uncomfortable.

A very popular preacher among the Brethren on the West coast commented on the ministry received growing up in the assemblies:

> The Bible teaching that we did get by those who were well thought of (those renowned, so to speak, all over this country) were people who spiritualized the Bible to the point where I have spent the last 30 years of my life unlearning the things I learned in the first 25. The Bible was not interpreted literally, but it was seen as an analogy. In actuality, the analogies were applications of the passage. But the applications were presented as interpretations. This has been my biggest struggle (as a full-time worker). I grew up thinking those applications were the actual interpretations of the passage.

Dissatisfaction with the Quality of Worship

One person in their late thirties, a third generation Brethren, made this statement about the communion service:

> I can go back to when I was child and I have to say that this meeting, regardless of what the scriptures may say about it, I have never enjoyed, except for the occasional time at camp when it was different.

Another third generation Brethren from a well-known Brethren family made this revealing comment:

> The Breaking of Bread over the years was a spooky, scary, sad and morbid meeting. It gave me eerie feelings. The only thing primarily discussed was the awfulness of the death of Jesus. . . . The Breaking of Bread was so cold and uncomfortable that it left a lot of unpleasant feelings in me.

An elder in a Chicago area assembly, speaking critically of the mournful nature of the worship service, noted:

> The phrase "in the night he was betrayed" is the mood setter. It is designed to take you into the Passion of our Lord and into the Garden experience. It's very mournful. The best remembrance meetings were those where there were tears or at least misty eyes. It reminds me of Robert Louis Stevenson's words, "I have been to church and I'm now sad."

A former elder from the Portland area made this statement:

> After three years I have finally gotten over the guilt trip of not being in an assembly and worshiping the way worship and Breaking of Bread are supposed to be. It has taken a long time.

Another former elder made this interesting comparison:

> There is an element that I miss in the Brethren worship; however, on the other hand in the Episcopal church, in this whole area of worship, there is actually more participation. There is participation in prayer together and worshiping together. This is done orally together with everyone participating. Admittedly, this is a different kind of participation but a real experience. It is becoming more meaningful all the time.

A dean of students of a Christian liberal arts college and former Brethren commented:

The Lord's Supper was supposed to be spiritually enriching or enhancing, but in my experience it was quite dead. We began visiting another church where they had the Breaking of Bread once a month. We were moved by that experience. It was spiritually an uplifting experience. When we began to compare and contrast that with our experience in the Brethren, we realized that our every-week experience was more like a ritual with no depth or positive experience. Inevitably, however, there was always one brother who would say that it was a moving experience. But I never felt that about the Breaking of Bread.

One potential leader, after being actively involved in the Brethren for 14 years, made this comparison:

After we had been visiting this church for about four or five Sundays and after we had experienced their worship and share time which, incidentally, allowed for open participation, we had an occasion to go back to our assembly and to the Lord's Supper. When they closed in prayer, I looked at my wife and said, "Can you believe the difference!" It just hit me between the eyes what life is all about, what enthusiasm for the Lord is all about. What a drastic contrast. The basic concepts for worship are there in both, but one has life and enthusiasm. The assembly doesn't.

Parochialism

A third generation ex-Brethren made this statement which illustrated parochialism.

When we went to the Baptist church, I was actually amazed that the people there were born again Christians. Do you see how narrow-minded I was? All because of the way I was brought up in the assemblies.

An academician from the East coast observed:

We never made a conscious decision to leave the Brethren. It was just a set of circumstances that forced us out. My wife's parents left and our own experience in other kinds of fellowships changed us. I was no longer under the understanding that the Brethren way of meeting was the one true way of meeting. This was the way I was brought up. The Brethren way was the Christ-intended way for the church to meet.

A commended worker from the Midwest made essentially the same observation:

> As a child growing up in the assemblies, we lived in such isolation from other Christian communities we had no way of comparing. Separatism was total. It was not until I went into the Army during WW II that I saw something seriously wrong with the fellowship I came from. To my surprise, I discovered Christians in other denominations were much more zealous and they seemed to know their Bibles better than me.

An elder and full-time worker from Northern California explained how he was programmed into narrowness:

> I grew up in a small assembly in the Midwest. There were no more than 50 people in the assembly. This fellowship was all one knew. Other Christians were commonly referred to as people who did not have the truth. They were gathered to denominational organizations as opposed to us who were gathered to the name of the Lord Jesus. They were not separated Christians as we were.
>
> I heard nothing but negative things about Christians in other churches. As a boy, it was imparted to me that though we were small, we were very special . . . The negativism in the Brethren is absolutely deathly. I have, just in the past few years, been aware of how negative I have been in my own thinking . . . Just recently the Christian world and the real world have opened up to me. I had a very restrictive world view. I am still in the Brethren movement, but I am on the edge looking out at a whole new world, including a new Christian world. I love the people in the Brethren, but I hate the system that so severely restricts one's world view.

Some ex-Brethren have even stronger feelings:

> I am really angry with the Plymouth Brethren movement because I feel I got conned. Looking back I think I was brainwashed into believing that no one can be characterized as a Christian outside of the Brethren. Everyone else was heretical. As a result, there is no place to go. I am most angry about what that did to my family. We hung in there in a dying assembly during the formative years of our children. It had its effects. I am not pawning off my responsibility of raising our family, but had we gone somewhere (another church) where we would have gotten real support for our children, I'm sure things would have been much different today. They needed a viable group of peers with whom to associate.

Another illustration of this parochialism, which is really uninformed arrogance, was heard in a Eastern city. When the elders learned that one of their promising young couples was about to leave the assembly, they approached David (the husband) and said:

> If you leave and go to one of the churches, you won't be involved in ministry anymore. You won't be able to teach and preach and your gifts will not be allowed to develop.

David's wife comments:

> But today David is an active elder teaching adults. We both sing in the choir. I teach a women's Bible study. David writes a ministry column every month for the church newsletter. We have a neighborhood Bible class in our home. Spiritually we are much more alive.

Another academician ex-Brethren was even more harsh in criticizing: "There is something cultish about the Brethren. From the inside it is very hard to see. But when you get away and look back objectively, you see things that are utterly unappealing. When asked to elaborte on these cultic tendencies, this person went on:

> First, I have never seen a freed assembly. By that I mean one that could accept self-criticism. The Brethren won't accept criticism. In some things, yes, but in others, no. Try criticizing worship. No way. Second, the authoritarian structure. Decisions are not made unless this one key person gives the okay. Third, many of the practices become concretized. No change, period. Fourth, there is intolerance for other fellowships. I have heard the comment, "That's the way they do it in *the* churches." A smug arrogance.

This was certainly the experience of one young intellectual who said:

> While I was getting my Ph.D. at Stanford, we were attending an assembly. I became gradually uncomfortable or unhappy with the level of understanding of the faith and the communicating of that faith. Another way of expressing what I'm trying to say is I have become uncomfortable with the way the whole Christian experience was viewed.... The straw that broke the camel's back happened one Sunday morning at the Family Bible Hour. A young man was speaking and he held up a psychology textbook in one hand and the Bible in the other. He said, "Here are your choices— man's wisdom (the psych text) or the Bible, God's wisdom." I quickly concluded there was another choice. I don't have to listen to this tripe.

A professional person made this observation:

As long as I can remember, there has been a strong anti-education attitude. This was especially seen in regards to theological training. It was simply unacceptable. . . . There has always been an under-current that education was bad.

A commended worker, reflecting upon the early days shortly after his commendation, said:

I received a negative attitude toward furthering my education in Christian things. I remember the attitude of those in the assembly toward those who were receiving training from Biola. They were looked upon as those who were usurping the ministry of the Holy Spirit. That attitude is still very strong even today.

In fact, a former Brethren said: "There is no question that those who have been educated, especially theologically, feel uncomfortable in many of the assemblies."

Note the following insightful comment:

The educated people in the Brethren movement that I have exper-ienced in New England are being pushed out or they have not felt support enough to stay in the movement. The main reason is their progressive ideas. These progressive ideas came as a result of edu-cation and understanding broader issues. One becomes less parochial. This causes friction because many of the assemblies that I'm familiar with are led by people who are quite unsophisticated and are quite fearful of what college has done to their kids or those they have heard about.

This kind of attitude goes against progressiveness. It seems to me you need progressiveness to engage in renewal. Without it, you cannot meet the needs of the people where they are. This anti-progressiveness is counterproductive because it cuts off the desire of young men and young women to express the idea of seeing needs and wanting to meet needs. They are told you can't do that because we do not do things like that.

This creates a great deal of frustration. The frustration level increases because the existing leadership wants so much to assert its authority and dominance. They are not willing to have open dialogue. Some are so fearful of allowing people to express issues in an open forum or discussion. So they would rather push people out.

The attitude is we do not need these kinds of hassles among us. We do not need these kinds of ideas infiltrating us. The consequences of this are that it produces ineffectual small groups.

Appendix B
An Assembly Questionnaire

This questionnaire was designed to aid the leadership of an assembly in evaluating its own spiritual condition and direction.

Please be candid and honest in your response. Additional comments are encouraged and will be appreciatively received. Your opinion is valued and will be carefully considered.

General Information

1. Sex:____male____female; Age group:____18-20,____21-24,
   ____25-29,____30-39,____40-49,____50-65,____over 65.

2. Educational level:____high school,____some college,
   ____bachelor degree,____graduate degree.

3. Income level:____0-$9,000,____$10,000-$19,000,
   ____$20,000-$29,000,____$30,000-$39,000,____$40,000-
   $49,000,____$50,000-$59,000,____$60,000-$69,000,
   ____over $70,000.

4. Married:____yes____no; Political preference:____Democrat,
   ____Republican,____Other

5. How long have you been attending this assembly?
   ____0-2 years,____3-5,____6-10,____over 10.

6. I attend the following regularly:____Breaking of Bread,
   ____Bible Fellowship Hour (11 AM),____Sunday School,
   ____Midweek Service.

7. I attend the following occasionally:____Breaking of Bread,
   ____Bible Fellowship Hour (11 AM),____Sunday School,
   ____Midweek Service.

8. How many miles do you travel to the assembly? ____0-2,
   ____2-5,____5-10,____10-15,____15-20,____20-30,
   ____over 30 miles.

9. I am or have been involved in:____teaching Sunday School,
   ____Junior Church,____youth sponsor,____D.V.B.S.,
   ____music ministry,____usher/greeter,____visitation,
   ____outreach evangelism,____leadership (elder/deacon),
   ____Other_____

COMMENTS:

Leadership and Congregational Purposes

Instructions: After each statement, circle the number that best describes your reaction to each statement.

		Strongly Agree	Agree	Disagree	Strongly Disagree	No Opinion
1.	The purposes of this congregation are clear to me.	1	2	3	4	5
2.	The purposes of this congregation are merely implied.	1	2	3	4	5
3.	My personal purposes are consistent with the purposes of this congregation.	1	2	3	4	5
4.	It is clear to me how we are moving to achieve our purposes.	1	2	3	4	5
5.	Our church programs are planned in accordance with our purposes.	1	2	3	4	5
6.	The elders present well the purposes I see for the church.	1	2	3	4	5
7.	I feel known and cared for by my elders.	1	2	3	4	5
8.	There is good communication between the elders and the congregation.	1	2	3	4	5
9.	It is a good idea to have a full-time worker and/or administrator.	1	2	3	4	5
10.	There is a need for occasional change in the eldership.	1	2	3	4	5
11.	There is a need for a broader representation on the eldership.	1	2	3	4	5
12.	There is at least one elder whom I would go to with my deep personal problems.	1	2	3	4	5
13.	I have respect and confidence in the leadership.	1	2	3	4	5
14.	One of the major responsibilities of the church is to	1	2	3	4	5

	Strongly Agree	Agree	Disagree	Strongly Disagree	No Opinion
minister to the physical as well as the spiritual needs of the congregation.					
15. The church has an obligation to help its members to minister to others in everyday life.	1	2	3	4	5
16. The church ought not get involved in controversial political issues (ERA, bussing, Moral Majority, etc.).	1	2	3	4	5
17. The church ought not get involved in controversial social issues (abortion, the poor, etc.).	1	2	3	4	5
18. I feel free to express to others in this church my views on controversial social and political issues even though many may disagree with me.	1	2	3	4	5
19. This church should belong to a local fellowship of other evangelical churches.	1	2	3	4	5
20. Sunday is too busy a day— we should cut down on our activities.	1	2	3	4	5
21. This church should unite with other evangelical churches for special evangelistic campaigns.	1	2	3	4	5
22. This church should unite with other evangelical churches concerning certain moral, social and political issues.	1	2	3	4	5

23. List what you feel are the purposes of this congregation:

The Lord's Supper

	Strongly Agree	Agree	Disagree	Strongly Disagree	No Opinion
1. The Lord's Supper reflects the worship desires of the majority of the congregation.	1	2	3	4	5

		Strongly Agree	Agree	Disagree	Strongly Disagree	No Opinion
2.	The Lord's Supper is regularly evaluated by the leadership.	1	2	3	4	5
3.	The Lord's Supper format provides for the kind of participation I like.	1	2	3	4	5
4.	There is an atmosphere of freedom and flexibility in the Lord's Supper.	1	2	3	4	5
5.	The hymns we sing reflect the preference of the congregation.	1	2	3	4	5
6.	The use of more musical instruments would enhance the Lord's Supper.	1	2	3	4	5
7.	There is a sense of expectancy and excitement at the Lord's Supper.	1	2	3	4	5
8.	There are elements in the Lord's Supper that need change.	1	2	3	4	5
9.	The length of the Lord's Supper is satisfactory.	1	2	3	4	5
10.	Change in the Lord's Supper would upset me.	1	2	3	4	5
11.	Women should not be allowed to participate verbally at the Lord's Supper.	1	2	3	4	5
12.	Women should wear a head covering at the Lord's Supper.	1	2	3	4	5
13.	Women should wear a head covering at all services on the Lord's day.	1	2	3	4	5
14.	I believe the Lord's Supper is usually characterized by true worship of the Lord.	1	2	3	4	5
15.	I personally experience a sense of the Lord's presence and effective worship at the Lord's Supper.	1	2	3	4	5

COMMENTS:

The Pulpit Ministry

	Strongly Agree	Agree	Disagree	Strongly Disagree	No Opinion
1. The ministry service reflects the desires of the total congregation.	1	2	3	4	5
2. The ministry service is regularly reviewed and evaluated.	1	2	3	4	5
3. There is flexibility and variety in the ministry service.	1	2	3	4	5
4. The congregation has a sense of expectancy and anticipation.	1	2	3	4	5
5. The music we sing reflects the preference of the congregation.	1	2	3	4	5
6. The ministry is constantly edifying spiritually.	1	2	3	4	5
7. There are elements in the ministry service that need change.	1	2	3	4	5
8. The length of preaching service is satisfactory.	1	2	3	4	5
9. An evangelistic appeal should be made at each ministry service.	1	2	3	4	5
10. The primary purpose of the ministry service should be to preach the gospel.	1	2	3	4	5
11. The primary purpose of the ministry service should be the edification of the believer through preaching the whole counsel of God.	1	2	3	4	5
12. It would not matter if the Sunday speaker belonged to a denomination as long as he is sound.	1	2	3	4	5

COMMENTS:

Finances

	Strongly Agree	Agree	Disagree	Strongly Disagree	No Opinion
1. I am satisfied with the amount of financial information which the elders provide to the congregation.	1	2	3	4	5
2. Our budget is too high for the number of contributors we have.	1	2	3	4	5
3. We should increase the percentage of our budget allocated for foreign missions.	1	2	3	4	5
4. We should increase the percentage of our budget allocated for home missions.	1	2	3	4	5
5. We should increase the percentage of our budget allocated for full-time workers.	1	2	3	4	5
6. More individuals and groups should be given a voice in establishing the budget.	1	2	3	4	5
7. There are some listed on our missionary budget whom I would hesitate to support financially.	1	2	3	4	5

COMMENTS:

Midweek Meetings

		Strongly Agree	Agree	Disagree	Strongly Disagree	No Opinion
1.	The midweek meetings reflect the desires of the total congregation.	1	2	3	4	5
2.	The midweek meetings are meeting my needs.	1	2	3	4	5
3.	The midweek meetings are regularly evaluated and reviewed.	1	2	3	4	5
4.	The midweek meetings provide the kind of participation I want.	1	2	3	4	5
5.	The midweek meetings are flexible and adaptable to the needs of those participating.	1	2	3	4	5
6.	The midweek meetings create cliques in the congregation.	1	2	3	4	5

COMMENTS:

Fellowship Climate (How It Feels Here)

The following pairs of words are opposite descriptions of an atmosphere. Check the space nearest the word that best reflects your feelings concerning the fellowship climate in your Assembly.

The Climate in this Assembly

alert	_____ _____ _____ _____ _____	not alert
mistrustful	_____ _____ _____ _____ _____	trustful
cooperative	_____ _____ _____ _____ _____	uncooperative
personal & close	_____ _____ _____ _____ _____	impersonal & distant
creative	_____ _____ _____ _____ _____	uncreative
insensitive	_____ _____ _____ _____ _____	sensitive
facing problems	_____ _____ _____ _____ _____	avoiding problems
conservative	_____ _____ _____ _____ _____	innovative
unconcerned	_____ _____ _____ _____ _____	concerned
listening	_____ _____ _____ _____ _____	not listening
fearful	_____ _____ _____ _____ _____	not fearful
rigid	_____ _____ _____ _____ _____	flexible
feelings ignored	_____ _____ _____ _____ _____	feelings count
divided	_____ _____ _____ _____ _____	unified
relaxed	_____ _____ _____ _____ _____	tense

COMMENTS:

Bibliography

Books

Arndt, William F., and Gingrick, F. Wilbur. *A Greek-English Lexicon of the New Testament.* Chicago: The University of Chicago Press, 1957.

Barclay, William. *The Letters to the Corinthians.* Edinburgh: The Saint Andrew Press, 1962.

Bass, Clarence B. *Backgrounds to Dispensationalism.* Grand Rapids: William B. Eerdmans Publishing Co., 1960.

Bettenson, Henry, ed. *Documents of the Christian Church.* New York: Oxford University Press, 1947.

Bloesch, Donald. *The Evangelical Renaissance.* Grand Rapids: William B. Eerdmans Publishing Co., 1973.

Bonhoeffer, Dietrich. *Life Together.* New York: Harper & Bros., 1954.

Bruce, F. F. "Lessons from the Early Church." In *God's Community,* pp. 153-168. Edited by David Ellis and Ward Gasque. Wheaton: Harold Shaw Publishers, 1979.

Carson, James C. L. *The Heresies of the Plymouth Brethren.* London: Paternoster Row, 1877.

Coad, F. Roy. "Prophetic Developments," *A Christian Brethren Research Fellowship Occasional Paper Number 2* Middlesex: CBRF Publication, 1966.

———— *A History of the Brethren Movement.* Exeter England: Paternoster Press, 1968.

Cook, Guillermo. *The Expectation of the Poor.* Maryknoll, NY: Orbis, 1985.

Darby, J. N. *Collected Writings of J. N. Darby.* ed. W. Kelly. London: Paternoster Row, reprint 1971.

Denzin, Norman K., ed. *Sociological Methods.* Chicago: Aldine Publishing Company, 1970.

Douglas, J. D., ed. *Let the Earth Hear His Voice.* Minneapolis: World Wide Publications, 1975.

Dulles, Avery. *Models of the Church.* Garden City, N.Y.: Doubleday & Co., 1974.

Fleming, Lois C. "A Pilot Study of Open Plymouth Brethren Assemblies in North America Responsive to Change." (Unpublished master's thesis, Wheaton College), 1984.

Foster, Richard J. *Celebration of Discipline.* New York: Harper & Row, 1978.

Green, Michael. *I Believe in the Holy Spirit.* Grand Rapids: William B. Eerdmans Publishing Co., 1980.

Hyde, Douglas. *Dedication and Leadership.* Notre Dame, Indiana: University of Notre Dame Press, 1966.

Ironside, H. A. *A Historical Sketch of the Brethren Movement.* Grand Rapids: Zondervan Publishing House, 1941.

Latourette, K. S. *Christianity in a Revolutionary Age. Vol. III: The 19th Century Outside Europe.* Grand Rapids: Zondervan Publishing House, 1970.

Liefeld, Walter. *In God's Community*. Wheaton, IL: Harold Shaw Publishers, 1979.

Lovelace Richard F. *Dynamics of Spiritual Life.* Downers Grove: Inter Varsity Press, 1980.

MacKintosh, C. H. *Miscellaneous Writings.* Neptune, N. J.: Loizeaux Brothers, 1966.

MacPherson, Dave. *The Incredible Coverup*. Plainfield, N.J.: Logos International, 1975.

Mallone, George. *Furnace of Renewal.* Downers Grove: Inter Varsity Press, 1981.

Martin, P. P. *The Epistle of Paul to the Philippians.* Grand Rapids: William B. Eerdmans Publishing Co., 1965.

_____ *The Worship of God.* Grand Rapids: William B. Eerdmans Publishing Co. 1982.

McDowell, Ian. *A Brief History of the Brethren.* Sydney, Australia: Victory Books, 1968.

McLaren, Ross. *The Triple Tradition: The Origin and Development of the Open Brethren in North America.* Ann Harbor: University Microfilms International, 1982.

MacPherson, Dave. *The Incredible Coverup.* Plainfield, NJ: Logos International, 1976.

Miller, Andrew. *Church History.* Grand Rapids: Zondervan Publishing House, 1964.

Minear, Paul S. *Images of the Church in the New Testament.* Philadelphia: The Westminster Press, 1960.

_____ "Church, idea of." In *Interpreter's Dictionary of the Bible.* pp. 607-617. Edited by G. Buttrick, et al. New York: Abingdon Press, 1962.

Neatby, William Blair. *A History of the Plymouth Brethren.* London: Hodder and Stoughton, 1901.

Niebuhr, Richard H. *Social Sources of Denominationalism.* Cleveland: World, 1957.

Noel, Napoleon. *History of the Brethren.* 2 Vols. Denver: W. F. Knapp, 1936.

Perry, Lloyd. *Getting the Church on Target.* Chicago: Moody Press, 1977.

Richards, Lawrence O., and Hoeldtke, Clyde. *A Theology of Church Leadership.* Grand Rapids: Zondervan Publishing House, 1981.

Rowdon, Harold H. *The Origins of the Brethren 1825-1850.* London: Pickering and Inglis, 1967.

Sandeen, Ernest R. *The Roots of Fundamentalism.* Chicago: University of Chicago Press, 1970.

Schaeffer, Francis A. *The Church at the End of the 20th Century.* Downers Grove: Inter Varsity Press, 1970.

Schwartz, Howard; Jacobs, Jerry. *Qualitative Sociology.* New York: The Free Press, 1979.

Sider, Ronald J. *Rich Christians in an Age of Hunger.* Downers Grove: Inter Varsity Press, 1977.

Snyder, Howard A. *The Problem of Wine Skins.* Downers Grove: Inter Varsity Press, 1975.

———— *The Community of the King.* Downers Grove: Inter Varsity Press, 1977.

Steer, Roger. *George Miller: Delight in God.* Wheaton: Harold Shaw Publishers, 1975.

Swindoll, Charles. *Strike the Original Match.* Portland: Multnomah Press, 1980.

Thompson, Kevin M. "A Manual for Small Group Ministry." In *Building Christian Community Through Small Groups,* p. 18a.

Watson, David. *How to Win the War.* Wheaton: Harold Shaw Publishers, 1979a.

———— *I Believe in Evangelism.* Grand Rapids: William B. Eerdmans Publishing Co., 1979b.

———— *I Believe in the Church.* Grand Rapids: William B. Eerdmans Publishing Co ., 1978.

———— *One in the Spirit.* London: Hodder and Stoughton, 1973.

Webber, Robert E. *Common Roots.* Grand Rapids: Zondervan Publishing House, 1978.

Young, Robert. *Analytical Concordance to the Bible.* Grand Rapids: William B. Eerdmans Publishing Co., 1955.

Articles, Pamphlets

Dinwiddie. "Music is a Contemporary Citizen." *Christianity Today.* September 3, 1982, pp. 96-97.

Groves, Anthony Norris. *The Basis of Christian Fellowship.* Edited by Keith Price. Montreal: Direction Publications, n.d.

Leech, Bryan J. "Truth, Taste and Tolerance." *Theology News and Notes.* March 1982, pp. 15-17.

McLaren, Ross. "His Appointed Way: Second thoughts on the Remembrance Meeting. *The Harvester.* November 1976.

Soltau, Henry W. *The Brethren, Who Are They? What Are Their Doctrines?* London: 1863.

Stunt, Timothy C. F. "Early Brethren & the Society of Friends." *Christian Brethren Research Fellowship Occasional Paper Number 3.* C.B.R.F. publication, 1970.

Miscellaneous

Anglican Lambeth Conference, Lambeth, England, July 1978.

California Center for Biblical Studies, 5441 Overland Avenue, Culver City, CA 90230.

Churches Alive, Box 3800, San Bernardino, CA 92413.

International Teams, P.O. Box 203, Prospect Heights, IL 60070.

Nathan DeLynn Smith, known to many as Nate or "Skip," graduated as an Academic All-American from UCLA. He turned down a professional contract with the Pittsburg Steelers to go to Dallas Theological Seminary. After graduating from Dallas he taught for four years at Emmaus Bible School and fourteen years at the California Center for Biblical Studies where he was the Academic Dean. In June of 1985, he graduated with a Doctor of Ministry degree from Fuller Theological Seminary. Currently, he is the President and Executive Director of a para-church organization involved in ministry to Christian businessmen, international students, as well as an active ministry in church planting and church renewal. He is practically involved in the local church, serving on the leadership of a growing assembly in Culver City, California. Presently he is writing another book on "Work and the Christian."

Order Form

ROOTS, RENEWAL AND THE BRETHREN

Hope Publishing House
P. O. Box 60008
Pasadena CA 91106

Please send me _____ **hardback** copies of

ROOTS, RENEWAL AND THE BRETHREN

@ $12.95 plus 95¢ for postage and handling for each book
   California residents add 6½% tax.
   (Order three or more copies and receive **free postage and handling.**)

Please send me _____ **paperback** copies of

ROOTS, RENEWAL AND THE BRETHREN

@ $6.95 plus 95¢ for postage and handling for each book
   California residents add 6½% tax.
   (Order five or more copies and receive **free postage and handling.**)

* *

Today's date is _____.

Mail books to: (Label—Please Print Clearly)

Name _____

Address _____

City, State, Zip _____

I enclose $_____ with this order.

Postage
Stamp

to: **Hope Publishing House**
P.O. Box 60008
Pasadena CA 91106